A Long Shot to Glory

*How Lake Placid Saved the Winter Olympics
and Restored the Nation's Pride*

Michael Burgess

Sister Joan —
I am glad we
have had a chance
to share some times
at this special place
we love Michael 12/8/12

First published by Dog Ear Publishing
4010 W. 86th Street, Ste H
Indianapolis, IN 46268
www.dogearpublishing.net

ISBN: 978-1-4575-1287-2

This book is printed on acid-free paper.

Printed in the United States of America

Table of Contents

Introduction

Sometimes life is like a movie. There are moments and events in life - not often - that are as exciting and as dramatic as a movie. What happened in Lake Placid, New York in February 1980 at the Thirteenth Winter Olympics was such a time. For those who experienced it in person or watched the games on television, they remember where they were when the US hockey team beat the Soviet Union and then beat the team from Finland two days later to win the gold medal. The sports victory of an underdog group of college kids was thrilling enough but it was a win against the Soviet Union. This Cold War adversary was also the nation hosting the summer games later that year which the United States was threatening to boycott.

The Lake Placid games were "home games" for the United States as well as for New York State, the first Olympics held in the country since the 8th Winter Olympics in Squaw Valley, California twenty years earlier in 1960. These games were in a quaint, storybook mountain village that wanted to play proud host and return the games to the athlete and back to a small town in the mountains with a legacy of winter sports and the Olympics.

When most Americans think of the 1980 Winter Olympic Games at Lake Placid, they remember that "Miracle on Ice." They also remember Eric Heiden, the American golden boy in his golden spandex who won five speed skating gold medals.

As 1980 US Olympic goalie Jim Craig wrote in the foreword to Wayne Coffey's *The Boys of Winter*,

"I don't believe those Winter Games in Lake Placid will ever be duplicated. I don't say it because we beat maybe the greatest Soviet hockey team ever assembled, or even because Eric Heiden won five gold medals, a performance that I honestly think dwarfs what we did. I say it because there weren't doping scandals or judging scandals or an Olympic Village that was overrun with millionaires and professionals in Lake Placid. Herb Brooks, God rest his soul, wasn't coaching a Dream Team. He was coaching a team full of dreamers. There is a big difference."

The Lake Placid games took place just as the United States threatened to boycott the Moscow Summer Olympics after the Soviet Union had invaded Afghanistan weeks before the opening ceremony. The games came at such an important moment in American history and provided a euphoria, a sense of patriotism and national pride at a time when the United States had endured more than a decade of self-doubt. The 1970s had been the decade with Vietnam and Watergate, an oil crisis, economic stagnation and it was ending with the humiliating Iranian hostage crisis. These events had erased the trademark American optimism, enthusiastic spirit and sense of goodness that propelled the postwar nation.

In many ways the 1980 Winter Olympics were one of those all too infrequent happy moments in a country's life when sheer joy overpowered all the negative news in the world and seemed to erase past frustrations. After the hockey victory, one spectator remarked that the Lake Placid Olympics were the best thing to happen to this country since the 1969 moon landing.

What happened on the hockey ice was improbable enough, but the entire games had been an improbable, decades-long quest for this small town to overcome the barriers of exploding finances, environmental concerns and world politics. The odds were against Lake Placid in its bids for the games and then it had so many obstacles to overcome to stage the games in its small town setting. Without the enthusiasm and perseverance of the leaders in Lake Placid and the professional support of New York State and an outside General Manager, the games of 1980 might have been cancelled altogether.

The Lake Placid Winter Games themselves were a longshot, if not a miracle themselves. The 1980 games were never supposed to take place in Lake Placid. They came to the small village because of unexpected events which unfolded and made the two weeks in the remote Adirondacks before a worldwide audience of nearly a billion viewers one of the most dramatic times in the modern era of sports, media and politics. The fact that the games did happen and ended with such euphoria in the United States was a tremendous boost to our own country and to the Olympic movement which was struggling under the cloud of international terrorism at Munich, financial excess in Montreal and the international boycott facing Moscow. In writing this book, I want to show that with so much bad news in the world, especially at that time, this was a brief shining moment of good news to be remembered and cherished with pride for the people of Lake Placid, New York State and the United States.

At the time many might have remembered some of the details about how the 1980 games came to Lake Placid, but as years have passed, they may have forgotten, except perhaps for the locals in upstate New York and other followers of Olympic sports.

While I attended the games and remembered the preparation, I have realized as I have researched the details of the events leading up to the games, it would not be too much of a stretch to say that the Lake Placid Games of 1980, which brought the "Miracle on Ice," saved the Winter Olympics in 1980 and strengthened them for the future.

The excitement and drama in Lake Placid gave the games a huge lift of enthusiasm and popularity when some had even come to believe that staging the games was no longer affordable for many communities and that perhaps the 1980 Winter Games should be cancelled entirely. Indeed, as the games began, a *US News and World Report* magazine story questioned whether the Lake Placid games were the "last Olympics."

There was a strong feeling that the US Olympic boycott of the Moscow games would doom the Olympics, especially if an effort was made to hold alternate games for those nations joining the boycott. Robert Kane, the former Cornell University Director of Athletics who became the United States Olympic Committee (USOC) President, testified before Congress in January 1980 that, "The Olympic Games will never be the same...I don't think the Olympics could be re-established" if the United States boycotted the Moscow games.

This book is about how the 1980 Winter Olympics in Lake Placid came about, the history and the politics in preparing for the games and what their impact was on the village and the country. Much has been written about the actual competition of the games and books and a movie have been made about the "Miracle on Ice." This book will look more closely at the other story, at the hurdles Lake Placid dealt with to win the games and then to prepare for them from November 1974 to February 1980.

This book will place the Lake Placid games in the context of the times and examine the international tensions between the United States and the Soviet Union which played such an important role at the games. It will focus on the impact the hockey victory and the games themselves had on the country and the Olympics. And, finally this book will examine what the lasting impact of these games have been on the Lake Placid and the North Country and the village's continuing relationship with the Olympic Games through the athletes who live there and continue to train for future Olympics.

It is about how a group of enthusiastic, sports-minded, community leaders made what legendary ABC sports broadcaster Jim McKay called an "audacious" bid to host the games in a small town and overcame all the controversies about the environment, finances and international politics.

Eric Heiden (Lake Placid Olympic Museum photo)

A Place So Beautiful

Over forty years ago, I first set foot in Lake Placid, New York on the Fourth of July weekend in 1971, just days after I graduated from Watertown High School. Watertown was two and a half hours to the southwest of Lake Placid. It was just a little outside the orbit of family day trips and weekend vacations we took when I was a kid. My family loved the Adirondacks and we would spend some weekends there and take day trips for summer holiday picnics. Those picnics were always just a little over an hour away at Cranberry Lake in the western end of the Adirondack Park.

I always felt like my world was transformed in that short car trip as we were leaving Watertown, a small city that was pretty flat on a plain near Lake Ontario. As we made our way northeast the terrain rose on Route 3 and we entered a land of streams and lakes and evergreens amidst the hills and mountains. The water was so clear at Cranberry Lake. I liked to find the most colorful stones and rocks on the bottom at the little public beach there which was in a mining area of the mountains.

Sometimes, we would venture further along Route 3 to Tupper Lake or Long Lake. As we went beyond Cranberry Lake and were closer to Tupper Lake, I would get excited as the mountains would get higher in front of us. As a kid, I had a feeling that I was going someplace more remote and more beautiful in the wilderness.

Of course, I had heard of Lake Placid, but it was a longer trip from home and we never really went for that kind of more crowded, mountain vacation. We would see cars returning with bumper stickers saying they had climbed Whiteface Mountain or had been to Ausable Chasm or the North Pole or Frontier Town, all of which were attractions on the other side of the Adirondacks, past Lake Placid.

On that first visit to Lake Placid in 1971, I loved the magnificent "high peaks." The forty-six peaks over 4000 feet aren't as lofty as the Rockies but are among the tallest in the northeastern United States. I also loved all the activity in the little village with its Main Street hugging one side of pristine Mirror Lake. Canoes and kayaks gently glided its surface with no gas motorboats permitted. I loved the history and old world aura of the Olympic Arena built for the 1932 Olympics which stood in the center of town and hosted ice shows all summer. On the walls in the back lobby were pictures of the kings and queens of past winter festivals. I was struck by a tribute plaque to the 1961 US figure skating team members who were killed in a plane crash returning from the world championships in Belgium. Inside the arena on those hot summer days it was cool as aspiring skaters practiced all summer, many hoping to be competitors or champions in the future.

To me, Lake Placid was an idyllic storybook mountain village like one read about in Christmas tales from the old world. Yes, it was kind of a "gingerbread" village as one writer described it. I felt even more remote when I was there, further away and deep in the mountains. Those were the days before the internet and cellphones and hundreds of cable television stations. Lake Placid evoked a European feel, or what I imagined it to be with its Alpine influence. The architecture of the churches was alpine and rustic. On the side of one of the stores on Main

Street facing the park and bandshell there were crests and insignias of the cantons of Switzerland. Over the years I met several people who were from Switzerland or central Europe who said that they visited the Lake Placid area or even moved there because it reminded them of home.

I liked not only the mountain charm of Lake Placid with its European feel but I also liked the fact that it is a small North Country town. Even though it wasn't that close to home, it was still the kind of North Country town I had experienced having been born in Massena and visited my relatives there often and then gone to college at St. Lawrence University in the small town of Canton.

After my first visit to Lake Placid, it was five years before I returned after graduating from St. Lawrence University and working in Watertown. I had a job and some money then and I decided to set off on my own for a vacation in the Adirondacks. By 1976, Lake Placid had been awarded its bid to host the 1980 Winter Olympics. I bought a green tee shirt with the Olympics rings that said "Lake Placid 1980." It still seemed a long way off then. In the years to follow, Lake Placid would become my special place where I would spend my vacations.

For me the 1980 Winter Olympics in Lake Placid was the most exciting public event of my young adult years. I know that for many of my Baby Boomer contemporaries who grew up in upstate New York, particularly in the Adirondacks and the North Country, it was clearly the highlight of those youthful years we look back on with nostalgia now, over thirty years later.

We had grown up on the other side of the New York State Thruway in the other New York, small towns that watched the world go by on television but rarely part of the news. Remote and isolated, we appreciated when anyone in politics and the media would visit or pay attention. Over twenty years earlier, the attention of the nation had briefly turned to the North Country when the St. Lawrence Seaway was dedicated in Massena in 1959 by Queen Elizabeth and President Eisenhower who sailed the river in the royal yacht, Brittania. In 1980, the whole world was coming to visit Lake Placid and the national and international media would descend on this special place of ours. For those who lived not just in the North Country but upstate New York as well, these were our "home games" on the international sporting stage.

By early 1979 I had moved to Albany and the sense of excitement about the coming games grew especially in upstate New York when tickets went on sale for the events. In my twenties making only a small salary, I couldn't afford to buy tickets for many of the events but I always liked ski jumping and bought tickets for that event. ABC Sports had famously showed a film clip of a ski jumper crashing as its Wide World of Sports program began every Saturday with the saying that the network spanned the globe to show "the thrill of victory and the agony of defeat."

My friends, Marcus Harazin and Barbara Goldstein, were with me and we were lucky our tickets were for the Monday at the start of the second week of the games. If they had been earlier we might never have made the event because of the incredible break-down in the bus transportation which left thousands stranded in the cold in the first several days. By the time we went, the bus transportation was running smoothly and we were able to drive to Keene and get a bus into Lake Placid.

Four nights later, when the United States which had not lost in the Olympic hockey competition would face off against the Soviet Union, I sat in my apartment on South Allen Street in Albany and watched an old, small, black and white television. The game had already been played when ABC's Jim McKay came on early in the evening to show it in primetime. He made it clear that the game was over but he would not reveal the result. The live crowds behind him left me thinking that something dramatic had happened and perhaps our American team of collegians had won.

I wrote in my journal at the time:

"I was jumping and stomping on the floor in the final seconds. With each goal, all three floors of the house were rattled and when the game ended and we incredibly beat the Russians, 4-3, my neighbors rushed up to meet in my apartment to share the joy. That gathering speaks for itself about the special excitement - the incomparable excitement -of the event. There has been no other sporting event like it for me. Indeed the whole country was moved."

I have now vacationed in Lake Placid every summer since 1976. When my wife, Kate, and I got married in 1985, I had the thrill of introducing her who was born in Queens and grew up in Westchester County to the beauty of Lake Placid. When our children came they would enjoy summer days there too.

I have sat on the shores of Mirror Lake and looked at the shops, stores and buildings on the other side with the mountains rising high behind them. On quiet and lazy summer afternoons after jumping in the refreshing mountain water, I can hear the church bells from the other side announcing that the afternoon was an hour older. Over all these years, Lake Placid has been a special place for me to enjoy the tranquility of nature and small town life and often restore myself on vacations.

Every time I go there, we have fun swimming, canoeing, hiking, taking photographs. Sometimes it is cold and gray and harsh and the clouds and mist will be so intense the mountains will disappear. Then, on another day, the sun will come out and the sky will clear and you can see the panorama of mountains so clearly. The beauty stuns and delights and leaves you in awe.

Chapter One

Quest for the 1980 Games

"If we didn't get it this time, we'd have been trying for 1984, '88, '92, '96 and 2000. We'd never stop trying because God meant the Olympic Games for Lake Placid and God meant Lake Placid for the Olympic Games. Sooner or later, it could not be avoided."

—Luke Patnode, Lake Placid Chamber of Commerce

In October 1974, when the Olympic Committee met in Vienna to decide where to the hold the 1980 games, the Olympics were in trouble. Just two years earlier, at the summer games in Munich, the Olympic movement which had tried so hard to keep the games free from politics had its worst moment. Eleven Israelis were taken hostage and killed in the athletes' village. The details were dramatically reported live on ABC by Jim McKay. Terrorism had intervened in a brutal way and security concerns preoccupied the International Olympic Committee. International tensions between countries had always hung over the games but violence at the Olympics had always been avoided until Munich. In the future no chances could be taken that terrorism could re-occur.

Despite their great popularity, the future of the Winter Olympics was especially tenuous. The Olympics had become a costly spectacle that was unlike the simpler athletic competitions of previous gatherings. There was a strong sentiment in the International Olympic Committee (IOC) against the growth and cost of the winter games. The games had changed beginning in 1968 in Grenoble, France where the cost was $250 million. Four years later in Sapporo, Japan, costs have been estimated at $750 million to one billion dollars. These extravaganzas were a far cry from the quaint games of the past.

There was also pressure to allow professionals to compete. Some countries were upset that government sponsorship of teams from the Soviet Union and other Communist countries, in particular, really made their athletes professionals in the sense of being able to participate in their sport full time with full financial backing. Canada was so upset about this situation that it boycotted the hockey competition at Sapporo and Innsbruck in 1976.

Security concerns, financial costs and environmental controversies were real threats to the future of the games. After Munich, the next Olympics, the 12th winter games, were scheduled to take place in Denver in 1976, bringing the games back to the United States for the first time since Squaw Valley, California hosted the winter games in 1960.

In May 1970, the International Olympic Committee (IOC) had met and chosen Denver to be the host city for the 1976 Winter Games, which would coincide with the Bicentennial of the United States as well as the Centennial of the State of Colorado's entry into the union. The award was a source of great pride to Colorado's political and business community. The organizing committee estimated the games would cost $14 million. Soon, though it was clear that the public did not have the same enthusiasm, fearing the costs and the possible damage to the environment.

1970 was the year of the first Earth Day and a growing environmental movement was rising with a strong presence in Colorado. At the same time, the state was growing and the suburbs of Denver were expanding and developing more land. Opponents began to mount a campaign against the games. Denver Mayor William McNichols went to the 1972 Winter Games in Sapporo, Japan to assure the International Olympic Committee that "only 1% of the people back home oppose the Olympics."

The mayor was proven out of touch with the reality of the opposition. With the state having the option for citizens to put referendums on the ballot, opponents organized a group known as Citizens for Colorado's Future and collected over 77,000 signatures, which was 25,000 more than needed to have a vote to commit state funding.

As the nation went to the polls in November 1972 to choose between President Richard Nixon and Democratic Senator George McGovern, Colorado voters also went to the polls to decide whether to spend $5 million on the games and thus, the fate of the 1976 Denver Olympics. Proponents of the games who included the state's business and political leaders spent over $175,000 in the campaign while opponents had a media budget of $2,100. However, 59% of the voters said "no" to spending state money to finance the Olympics. Just a week later, Denver became the only city ever awarded the games to withdraw. It lost its chance to be the center of world attention for the 1976 games. The voters' rejection in Colorado only added to the sense that the Olympic games had become too big and costly.

Lord Michael Killanin, the President of the IOC, said that the rejection by Denver was a threat to the continuation of the winter games. There was a hostile sentiment among some committee members to the winter games because of their huge costs and the push to allow professionals to participate. In fact, the recently departed IOC President, Avery Brundage who had competed in the 1912 summer games in Stockholm, was a purist about the

Olympics and very doctrinaire about maintaining amateur athletics as the focus of the games. He felt some skiers were paid professionals and remarked when the games were first awarded to Denver that he hoped, "the Winter Olympics receive a decent burial in Denver....this poisonous cancer must be eliminated without further delay."

In 1972, Brundage was ending his twenty year reign as IOC President and was credited with his fierce dedication to the Olympic ideal which, to him, was able to unite peoples of many countries despite the wars and opposing ideologies and systems of government which divided people. He said it was "the greatest social force of our time." He ended his tenure with his controversial decision to resume the Munich games after the memorial for the slain Israelis.

In the past he was accused of racism for his insensitivity to banning the all-white Rhodesia team from participating in the Olympics. In the 1930s he was accused of pressuring American coaches to replace two Jewish athletes on the track team at the Berlin Olympics so as not to embarrass Adolf Hitler. He said even in 1971, "The Berlin Games were the finest in modern history...I will accept no dispute over that fact." He also opposed women being in the Olympics saying, "I am fed up to the ears with women as track and field competitors." If Brundage had had his way, there would have been no 1980 winter games. His successor, Lord Michael Killanin, did not have the same rigid views.

Killanin became President of the IOC in 1972 after serving as head of the Olympic Council of Ireland and representing the country on the IOC since 1952. He had sat as a member of the British House of Lords since 1927.

The United States Olympic Committee (USOC) had to select a new location as its replacement community to host the 1976 games. A month after Denver withdrew, Lake Placid voters

Lord Michael Killanin, President, International Olympic Committee, 1972-1980 (Lake Placid Olympic Museum photo)

approved an expenditure of $10,000 for a study to consider an Olympic bid. Meeting on January 4, 1973, the USOC would be considering Lake Placid and Salt Lake City. Lake Placid's supporters felt confident of getting the designation because much of the infrastructure already existed in Lake Placid from the 1932 winter games and Salt Lake City would have to build everything in three short years. In addition, political leaders in Utah were hesitant to support state funding for the games while New York Governor Nelson Rockefeller had already pledged state support for the games and had made presentations to the USOC to try to secure the games in prior years.

It was quite shocking to the Lake Placid bid group when Salt Lake City was designated to be the US Olympic Committee's official choice for the 1976 Winter games to bid against Innsbruck, Austria and Chamonix, France which also had held the games before and Tampere, Finland which hadn't. Financing would be key. Salt Lake City tried in the next few weeks before the International Olympic Committee met in Lausanne, Switzerland to get a commitment of funding from the US government but Congress wouldn't move that fast. By January 30, Salt Lake followed Denver and withdrew its bid.

After Salt Lake City withdrew, Lake Placid immediately went to work again and now was requested by the US Olympic Committee to make a bid in Lausanne, Switzerland to try to salvage the games for the United States. Garry "Bunny" Sheffield one of the group that went to Lausanne, distributed "Follow Me to Lake Placid" bumper stickers on a train from Zurich to Lausanne, according to Howard Riley, a reporter with the *Adirondack Enterprise* who was on that trip. It was too late to put it all together though. Innsbruck had more time to develop its proposal and it still had all the facilities from the 1964 Games it had successfully hosted. Even though Lake Placid had an infrastructure of some facilities which could be used, it still would need to get commitments of state and federal money as well.

Innsbruck won the IOC vote though a strong minority voted in favor of cancelling the winter games altogether. Innsbruck's victory came despite an impressive presentation by Rev. Bernard Fell, the President of the Lake Placid bid committee. Fell related the love and enthusiasm that he and the members of the Lake Placid bid committee had for the winter games saying, "40 years ago, Lake Placid hosted the third Olympic Winter Games... The Olympic flag was raised in that economically troubled time in our community... And gentlemen, that flag has never come down...with pride we have flown it ever since." Before they left, Lord Killanin said, "Keep in mind we'll be looking forward to seeing you people with a bid for 1980."

The International Olympic Committee would meet again just a little over a year and half later in October 1974 to vote for the selection of the 1980 games host city. Lake Placid had been invited by the IOC to submit a bid as were other prospective candidate cities. The Town of North Elba, which included the Village of Lake Placid, held two public hearings and a referendum was put to the voters to approve $20,000 for the preparation of the bid. The vote easily passed by a 726-576 margin.

In February 1974 President Richard Nixon sent a personal aide to hand a note to Lord Killanin. The President wrote:

On behalf of the American people, I cordially invite the International Olympic Committee to stage the 13th Winter Games in Lake Placid, NY. As a small, mountainous winter sports community and as the site of the 1932 Winter Games and numerous world championships, Lake Placid has both the rich tradition and demonstrated ability to conduct the 1980 Winter Games with quality and distinction. ... I take special pride, therefore, in extending to you and all the men and women of the Olympic movement a welcoming hand and the warm hospitality of the people of the United States for winter competition at Lake Placid in 1980."

In September, the USOC met in Milwaukee and officially selected Lake Placid as the United States entry to bid for the 1980 games. After Denver's withdrawal, the IOC had set "extraordinary" conditions for a bid from a United States community. It had to have proof of local support from citizens which the Lake Placid referendum provided. It also had to either have adequate facilities or commitments to finance new construction. There had been a joint resolution of support from the New York State Legislature as well as the letter from President Nixon. The IOC also insisted after Denver, that all future Olympic hosts had to pay a bond and sign a contract committing to the games.

Lake Placid would make a realistic presentation that *Sports Illustrated* described, "It is probable that there has never been an Olympic bid better prepared and more soundly based that the one Lake Placid brought to Vienna." Lake Placid had other assets that the IOC recognized. Though it was a small, remote area, it was within a day's drive of the largest population centers in the country. The winter climate for snow was considered the best in the eastern United States. And, the village and its leaders had, as Rev. Fell said, an intense appreciation for winter sports and the Olympics themselves and hosted numerous international sports competitions in the past after the 1932 games. It had also sent competitors on every United States team to all the winter games.

Rev. Bernard Fell, President Lake Placid Olympic Organizing Committee (Lake Placid Olympic Museum photo)

Four other cities were bidding for

the 1980 games, including Vancouver, Canada, Oslo, Norway, Chamonix, France, and Garmisch-Partenkirchen, in West Germany. As the IOC meeting approached in Vienna, the European cities withdrew their bids because of financial concerns, leaving only Vancouver and Lake Placid. Then, Vancouver withdrew after it concluded it could not get a commitment of the necessary funding. A late bid by Quebec City, Canada was also withdrawn. Lake Placid's committee was confident that their bid would be ratified at the upcoming IOC meeting despite some concern that the IOC could re-open the bidding process or simply cancel the 1980 games.

When the IOC convened in Vienna for the vote on October 27, 1974, Lake Placid sent 72 persons to the meeting to help with the presentation. Leaders who made the bid presentation were Robert Krumm, President of the United States Olympic Committee, State Senator Ronald Stafford who represented the Adirondack region, Luke Patnode, Mayor Robert Peacock, Rev. J. Bernard Fell, and Ronald MacKenzie. Lake Placid promised to have a smaller scale games "in perspective," which would be given back to the athletes instead of the growing commercial spectacles. Organizers felt that the IOC had been awarding the games to big cities which required some of the competitions had to be held a considerable distance away. In Lake Placid's bid plan, the venues for the games would be held right in the village, nestled in the mountains and at some venues just a few miles away.

For Lake Placid, this was its only hope. It could not offer to hold a costly extravaganza like those held in preceding years and could not accommodate a larger event than planned in its bid. Lake Placid won by default, winning the vote even though there were still committee members who were against even staging the Games at all in 1980. The decision by the IOC was viewed as a shift, an endorsement to return the games more to the athletes.

Meanwhile, Los Angeles was hoping to team with Lake Placid like it did in 1932 to host the summer games. It had been a custom in the early games for the same country to host both the summer and winter games in the same year, but Moscow was the favorite and proved to be the winner. After the vote, Mayor Peacock hugged the Moscow Mayor and held a little party. That night, there was little sense of the Cold War that would again become tense five years later between the two countries as 1980 dawned and the Olympic games were set to take place. On that October night, the long dream of the host committee, the "North Country Boys," as they were known locally, to return the Games to Lake Placid for the second time was realized in Vienna when the IOC met.

Chapter Two

Lake Placid and Its Winter Sports Heritage

"It was natural for a young man in Lake Placid to take up speed-skating. Every young fellow in the town was a speed skater. I thought if I could win an Olympic event it would be the highlight of my life."

— Jack Shea, 1932 Olympic speedskating gold medalist

L ong before the worldwide fame of the Olympics, it was the incredible beauty of the mountains and the setting of the village between two crystal clear lakes that beckoned city dwellers and other tourists to Lake Placid. The famed Lake Placid Club was founded in the 1890s by Melvil Dewey who also developed the Dewey Decimal System for classifying library books. Sitting on the shores of pristine, Mirror Lake, the Club became a popular summer tourist destination. Dewey felt it could also be a destination for winter recreation and he began to introduce skating and skiing at the club. In describing the history of winter sports in Lake Placid, the 1932 report on the games described those early years, "People had to almost literally to be taught how to enjoy winter, and they had to be given facilities with which to make that enjoyment complete."

Mirror Lake would be shoveled in front of the resort for their skating rink. Later, the Club began to hold winter sports competitions. They held the Eastern Skating Championships in 1918 on an eight lap track on Mirror Lake. It built a 35 meter ski jump at Intervale just outside Lake Placid and the first event was held there on February 21, 1921.

The Lake Placid Athletic Club had been formed to promote training and competitions. The village became known for its competitive skaters. The Lake Placid Skating Association had 273 members by 1920. In the 1920s Lake Placid had become the nation's premier winter sports resort and its athletes were participating in their first international competitions. Years later, Jack Shea would remember that in those years Lake Placid had become "the Switzerland of North America."

When the ancient Olympic games were re-instituted in Athens in 1896, the sports competitions were only for summer sports. Winter sports had been played mostly in the Scandinavian countries which had their own competitions. Those countries did not see a need for a worldwide winter Olympics since so few other countries had teams. At the London Summer games in 1908, an ice skating competition was held. The IOC authorized a winter sports competition in 1924 in Chamonix, France and it was later designated as the first Winter Olympics. Lake Placid's Charles Jewtraw, who had won the North American speed skating championship in 1921, captured what would be America's first Olympic gold medal in those first winter games.

In 1927, Dewey's son, Godfrey had inquired about whether Lake Placid could be considered for an Olympic bid. He later got a call from the International Olympic Committee inviting Lake Placid to bid for the 1932 Winter Games. So, in 1928, he made a trip to Europe to study how the games were conducted previously in Chamonix and he also attended the Second Winter Games in St. Moritz, Switzerland. He decided that Lake Placid had the ability to host the Olympics. However, when he returned and described his proposal to bid to host the games in 1932 to local leaders, they thought the idea was ridiculous and were opposed. Dewey kept talking about how Lake Placid had the ability to be as good as St. Moritz in hosting the games and he convinced them. The Lake Placid Chamber of Commerce voted on April 3, 1928 to go ahead with its bid and Dewey sailed to Europe and arrived in Lausanne, Switzerland to present the proposal with a $50,000 fee.

Los Angeles was chosen to host the 1932 Summer Games and several other cities and regions in the United States bid for the winter games including Lake Tahoe and Yosemite, California, Duluth, Minnesota and Bear Mountain, New York. Dewey had studied all the issues involved and he knew he had the best plan. It came down to California and Lake Placid but Dewey's presentation won. As the *New Yorker* magazine reported in 1932, "He took a lot of figures, statistics and photographs with him and, according to one member of the committee, he harangued, 'talked 'em dizzy'." The bid was awarded on April 10, 1929.

The Organizing Committee had great difficulty getting the money for the games during the Great Depression, so the construction of Olympic facilities at that time, including the new arena and the bobsled course, were an economic stimulus to the region.. Godfrey Dewey donated a plot of land on the Lake Placid Club property to be the site for the bobsled run. The Olympic Arena was built on Main Street in just five months for a cost of $220,000 and opened in January 1932. The games cost $1,137,654. The residents of Lake Placid would take about thirty years, into the early 1960s, to pay off the $350,000 debt.

E.B. White wrote in the *New Yorker* about the magic and charm of a more remote Lake Placid in that earlier, simple era, of the 1932 Olympics:

"The first moment, of course had been the best - the moment of raising the Pullman shade and seeing a white land. The train gets in early to

Placid, when the light is flat and the mountains invisible. Soon, the light strengthens, the valleys round out, up come the hills like clouds and you hear again a sound that has almost gone out of life - a sound that ought to be perpetuated somehow, the sound of sleighbells."

And he would sum it up,

"Occasionally in the midst of things there would come lucid moments: at the outskirts of town at dusk when the snow was blue and the sky like a backdrop, homebound skiers shuffling along, a town boy homebound from the grocery store dragging two loaves of bread on a little sleigh. And beyond the prowess of the athletes, the mountains, cold and unathletic, higher than the nations, colder than defeat, sane as anything."

The village welcomed the Winter Games and decorated itself with thousands of flags of the participating countries on Main Street. The *Lake Placid News* described the appearance of the village:

"Ice from mountain lakes and pine from the Adirondack woods form arches spanning entrances to public buildings, hues of varied colored lights shining through the ice colors in rainbow opalescence...hundreds of lights blaze nightly from evergreens decorating the porches of cottages, signaling a welcome to Olympic athletes and guests. Thousands of flags hung downtown and some businesses were covered from basement to roof with banners. Ropes of pine linked street lights and evergreens adorned intersections."

In the village of 2930 people, the 1932 Games were opened by New York Governor Franklin D. Roosevelt on February 4-15, 1932. 58,000 spectators would view the games which were broadcast on radio for the first time. Housing was available for 10,000 visitors within 60 miles at a rate of $3 to $7 per day and included 25 railroad sleeping cars in the village. Grandstands had been built for the opening ceremonies but they were less than half filled in those Depression days.

Jack Shea, a 21-year-old speed skater from Lake Placid who was a sophomore at Dartmouth took the athletes oath. Godfrey Dewey introduced "His Excellency," Governor Franklin D. Roosevelt who was supposed to just recite the official words opening the games. Roosevelt instead abandoned the protocol and made a plea for world peace, "I wish in these later days that the Olympic ideals of 2800 years ago could have carried out in one further part. In those days, it was the custom every four years, no matter what war was in progress to cease all obligations of armies during the period of the games. Can those early Olympic ideals be revived throughout all the world so that we can contribute in a larger measure?" At that time, Japan had invaded China and fighting did not stop and was raging throughout the games.

1932-1980

Jack Shea receiving gold medal from IOC President Count de Baillet-Latour 1932 Winter Games, Lake Placid (Lake Placid Olympic Museum photo)

Eleanor Roosevelt, accepted an invitation from one of the Lake Placid bobsled drivers to take a trip on the bobsled run. Seven persons had been injured on the run. Admiral Richard Byrd who had explored the South Pole also took the plunge. He was at the games looking for hardy souls who would like to join his future polar explorations.

There were 252 athletes, 231 men and 21 women, who came from seventeen countries - Austria, Belgium, Canada, Czecho-slovakia, Finland, France, Germany, Great Britain, Hungary, Italy, Japan, Norway, Poland, Rumania, Sweden, Switzerland and the United States - who participated in fourteen events in four sports: speed skating, hockey, figure skating and bobsled. The athletes paraded in following their country's placard. The Italians gave Mussolini's fascist salute as they passed Governor Roosevelt.

Western Union teletype operators sent 115,000 words out a day. The transmissions reached London in three minutes with the results and in no more than 10-15 minutes, the results were known in Japan. 85 journalists provided the radio and newspaper coverage of the games, which gained international fame for Lake Placid but the Depression tempered any sense of the village being overrun by land and business speculators.

In those difficult economic days before the Olympics were as popular as today, the public did not attend in overwhelming num-bers. A bus from Watertown to Lake Placid was supposed to run on two days for the games. It only ran on a Friday because of a lack of interest. The *Syracuse Post Standard* reported that the Lake Placid Club announced that were plenty of accommoda-tions and tickets available for those who still wanted to attend. The only sellout crowd in the arena was the 5000 persons for the ladies figure skating finals which were won by Sonja Henie, the young Norwegian star and reigning Olympic champion who won the gold in 1928 at St. Moritz. New York City's Mayor Jimmy Walker attended the games and watched her medal winning per-formance.

Speed skating took place at an oval in front of the Lake Placid High School. "American" style group skating took place rather than the European style of racers skating in pairs against the clock. Lake Placid's Jack Shea and Irving Jaffee were the hometown heroes as Shea won the 500 meter and 1500 meter men's speed skating gold medals. Shea returned to a hero's welcome at Dartmouth with a parade and bands playing. Jaffee, the son of poor immigrant parents won the 5000 meter and the 10,000 meter races. He worked as a messenger on Wall Street for $16 a week. His employers gave him a party when he returned and a gift of a gold watch. "And in that old Ingersoll watch, was two thousand dollar bills. Now, $2,000 in 1932, the Depression days, well, I was ready to buy the Woolworth building," he said.

After having hardly any snow all winter, the games closed in a blizzard, "A crowd of 5000 people hurried from the arena to see the closing ceremonies but soon thinned out, unable to stand the onslaughts of the biting blasts." Count de Baillet-Latour, President of the International Olympic Committee (IOC) issued a statement upon leaving the United States, "The thanks of the International Olympic Committee are due the community of Lake Placid for taking on in the III Olympic Winter Games of 1932 a greater burden in proportion to its size than any community ever assumed in staging Olympic contests."

The games closed with a call to the youth of the world to assemble again four years later in 1936 in Germany where both the summer and winter games would be held. Little did those in attendance in Lake Placid know that those games would take place in a Nazi Germany, which would plunge the world into war. After the summer games in Berlin in 1936 there were no Olympic games until after the Second World War in 1948.

Lake Placid lived on its fame and was still a destination for the wealthy in the years after 1932. An annual Winter Carnival and ice shows with big stars like Henie were staged at the Olympic arena in the 1940s and 1950s. Nationally known entertainers including Perry Como, Roy Rogers and Kirk Douglas were among those crowned as Kings of the Carnival. In the early part of the twentieth century Lake Placid had been home to composer Victor Herbert and singer Kate Smith who is buried there. She had owned a home and radio studio on Buck Island in the middle of Lake Placid. She was very active at St. Agnes Church and left part of her estate to it.

Lake Placid became known for its figure skating program which was led by famed coach Gustave Lussi. Most aspiring Olympic competitors came to the village to train and the village became known as the figure skating capital of America. Among Lussi's skating stars who went on to win the Olympic gold medal were Dick Button and later Dorothy Hamill in 1976. Some of the other skaters he coached were Barbara Ann Scott, John Curry, and Hayes Jenkins.

As auto travel became more common with the expansion of four lane interstates including the Adirondack Northway in the 1970s and as Americans became more affluent after World War II, Lake Placid became a popular middle class summer vacation spot. By the 1970s it had some newer chain hotels which could host large meetings of regional and statewide groups.

After World War II, a new middle class of civic minded leaders in the Chamber of Commerce promoted Lake Placid as a tourist location and sports venue. This group of local boosters typified small town post war America. Filled with civic pride for the community where most had grown up they volunteered in local organizations and supported community efforts. "They were raised on small town notions of neighborliness, loyalty and something elusive and old fashioned called community spirit," *Sports Illustrated* observed in an article after Lake Placid won the 1980 games.

They became known as the "North Country boys," local men who were civic promoters who felt that the sports history and beauty of Lake Placid made the village the right place for the games to return as they did to St. Moritz, Switzerland for the second time in 1948 after World War II ended.

This group of sports enthusiasts would set their sights on the dream of returning the Winter Olympics to Lake Placid. A key figure who had led the effort to get the Olympics back was Ronald MacKenzie, the former postmaster who had founded the Lake Placid ski club in 1921 and had been on the US bobsled team at the 1936 games in Garmisch-Partenkirchen, Germany. Norman Hess, a local attorney was a key sparkplug who was always pushing community leaders to try for the games again. Luke Patnode was the publicity director for Essex County who served as the leader of the bid committees on four occasions. He was another of the town's biggest cheerleaders. He said "There is not much we don't know about the ins and outs of Olympics - politically, technically, esthetically...it has been a way of life for most of us for years."

Another key leader of the group was Rev. Bernard Fell, a former police officer who was wounded in a shooting and then went on to become a Methodist minister Rev. Fell would become the Executive Director and later the President of the Lake Placid Olympic Organizing Committee (LPOOC). He would write in the program of the 1980 closing ceremonies, "Lake Placid is a community dedicated to sport...From their early years, the children of Lake Placid develop the skills that have produced six Olympic champions and at least one person from our tiny community on every United States Olympic team since 1924."

Vern Lamb was another leader of the bid committee. He, like Shea, went to Dartmouth. He owned Lamb Lumber Company in Lake Placid and was active in many community organizations. He served for a time as president of the Chamber of Commerce. He passed away in late 2011 and his son, Joe, who was on the 1972 US Olympic ski team, is now running the family business. He said his father was one who "didn't take the credit - he did things because they were right."

The group also included Jack Shea, Serge Lussi, the son of skating coach Gustav Lussi, and Art Devlin who was on the ski jumping team at the 1952 and 1956 games. Devlin was known as "Mr. Lake Placid." He was the best known publicly of the group since he was an ABC Sports Olympic commentator and always talked about his hometown. Devlin flew fifty combat missions in World War II over Europe and was a fixture in the community who ran a local motel on Main Street. Other North Country boys were Favor Smith, a town justice, Mayor Robert Peacock, and community leaders Phil Wolff, Bernie Alder, Gene Wilson, Gary "Bunny" Sheffield, Bob Allen and Shirley Seney, supervisor of the Town of North Elba.

Lake Placid had actually bid for the Winter Games almost every chance it had. It would make five bids, beginning in 1948 when the games were resumed after World War II. Over the years the North Country boys would travel with their bids to the IOC meetings and, despite rejection, they would continue to befriend and "lobby" members of the IOC.

St. Moritz was chosen for the 1948 games because Switzerland had been a neutral country during World War II and had also not sustained damage. Lake Placid tried again in 1952 but Oslo was chosen. The village added its winter bid on Detroit's bid for the 1956 summer games but both lost to Melbourne and Cortina D'Ampezzo, Italy.

Lake Placid had been handicapped by the lack of a major alpine skiing venue. That sport had not been part of the 1932 Olympics in Lake Placid but it was added four years later in Garmisch-Partenkirchen, Germany. In the 1940s, a ski center at Marble Mountain, part of Whiteface, was developed but it was not in the league with venues in other ski resorts in the United States or the facilities used by other Olympic cities.

Finally, in 1958, New York State helped build a ski center at Whiteface Mountain. It would also enhance Lake Placid as a winter sports resort and increase its prospects to bid for future Olympics. New York Governor Averill Harriman was an avid skier and previously, as President of the Union Pacific Railroad, had spearheaded the development of the Sun Valley, Idaho ski resort. He led the effort to amend the "forever wild" section of the state constitution and get $2.5 million in state dollars approved for Whiteface and took part in the opening of the facility in January 1958. He made national news when he got stuck on the chairlift on the mountain when it unexpectedly stopped.

By the early 1960s, *Sports Illustrated* would write an article about the 1932 Olympics and their goal of making Lake Placid an international winter sports mecca. It actually had been that with all the ice shows and other events but the magazine said that more had been expected, "Lake Placid never really caught on."

The North Country boys shared that feeling too. They expressed concern about the future of the community and its depressed economy. In the early 1960s, the village's prospects began to look brighter as it looked ahead to the 1968 Winter Games. It had the backing of Governor Nelson Rockefeller, a name well known to the IOC. Lake Placid secured the favored position as the official candidate of the United States Olympic Committee (USOC) for the 1968 Games and thought it had a real shot. It only got three votes though, as the games were awarded in 1964 to Grenoble, France. One member of the Olympic committee, explained his vote saying, "You just had the games in 1932." Then, the 1972 games were awarded to an Asian country for the first time with the choice of Sapporo, Japan, a city that had previously been awarded the games for 1940 but which were cancelled by World War II.

In March 1967, Lake Placid again submitted a bid to the USOC to host the 1976 Olympics. Salt Lake City, Denver, Seattle and Vermont would also bid. Governor Nelson Rockefeller made a strong presentation for Lake Placid at the USOC meeting in

New York City but Denver was chosen over Lake Placid, 26-17 on the final ballot after the others were eliminated.

Despite the rejections, Lake Placid leaders sought other opportunities to host national and international competitions. In January 1969, Lake Placid hosted the Kennedy Memorial Winter Games which were established in memory of President John F. Kennedy and his brother, Senator Robert F. Kennedy, to honor their commitment to physical fitness. $2 million was spent to upgrade the 1932 facilities and 300 athletes attended. The village also hosted the world bobsledding championships in 1949, 1961, 1969 and 1973.

By the 1970's Lake Placid was a small, one stoplight North Country town whose Olympic fame and glory seemed long passed but still visible with the old 1932 Olympic Arena near the center of the village on Main Street. Tourists across the Northeast, Canada and the United States trekked to the beautiful setting in the summer. They posed for photos with the pile of "snow" in front of the arena, which was really ice shaved off the rink used by skaters year-round.

It was in 1972 though that Lake Placid's fortunes dramatically turned. The village gained major international attention again and became a serious competitor for the Olympics. It won a bid to host the winter edition of the World University Games, which was the largest amateur international sporting event other than the Olympics. 500 athletes from 23 countries participated in 27 events. The games were a success and proved that Lake Placid could again host a major international sporting competition. With the staging of that successful event and Denver's demise later that year as host of the 1976 games, the North Country boys finally had a clear path to win the bid selection to host the winter games.

Forty-six years after he set sail for Switzerland to bid for the 1932 games, Godfrey Dewey, at age 87, lived to see the IOC award the winter games to Lake Placid a second time in 1974. He died at the age of 90 in October 1977, before the 1980 games. Upon his death, members of the Lake Placid committee called him "the father of winter sports in America."

Chapter Three
Land Mines

"It was the largest event held in the smallest place."
—Petr Spurney, General Manager, 1980 Winter Olympics

The selection of Lake Placid, aided by some luck, was a great achievement and source of pride for the North Country Boys and the entire community. Lake Placid relished its victory like it had won a political election. Then, like the hard task of governing, Lake Placid, would have to pull the games off in a little over five years from that night in Vienna.

The North Country boys had promised to hold an "Olympics in perspective." The idea of holding the games in a small town had seemed ill-advised as the games grew.. However, choosing a small town and smaller scale games had become more plausible after the financial, environmental and political problems plaguing other hosts and bidders. Lake Placid wanted to return the games to athletes and the competition rather than the selling of the competition. "The Olympics were becoming a spending event," Ronald MacKenzie told *US News and World Report* magazine in 1978. "It was just getting too expensive to hold the Olympic Games in a big city. Our feeling was, it should revert to what it once was - a contest among athletes - and we felt a small village like ours could provide a better setting than any city."

Lake Placid's committee said it could hold the games on a smaller, less costly scale than the Sapporo games in 1972. When Lake Placid's bid was finally approved, it estimated total costs had grown from an original estimate of $22 million to at least $35 million. Of course, there were many who doubted that the games could truly be conducted with such a limited budget and the costs in Lake Placid would dramatically escalate.

"It has come to be a fundamental fact of pre-Olympic life that organizing committees inevitably find themselves in trouble," *Sports Illustrated* wrote one year before the games. Lake Placid would be no exception. The Olympics are always filled with "land mines." In fact, it didn't take long before the path to the games would be strewn with these land mines and roadblocks. The cloud of Denver hung over Lake Placid's future games in the mid-1970s as there were constant threats and even suggestions that Innsbruck could be ready if needed again to step in at the last moment. When environmentalists began to challenge the impact of some proposed construction for the games, some members of the IOC wondered if the Lake Placid games would be derailed.

The little village of about 2800 people would need to be transformed even with the smaller scale of games planned. In the years from late 1974 until the beginning of 1980, the village would have to undertake more construction than it had seen in its history. Lake Placid would have to build or renovate facilities for the eight sports to be contested in 1980: speed skating, figure skating, hockey, biathlon, downhill skiing, ski jumping, bobsled and luge. A new Olympic arena for hockey and figure skating would have to be built along with two new ski jumps which would be the tallest structures between Albany and Montreal. The bobsled and luge runs would have to be refurbished. An outdoor speed skating oval would also be refrigerated in front of the Lake

Placid High School adjacent to the old arena and new Olympic arena.

A temporary stadium for the opening ceremonies would need to be built and an athletes' village would be constructed to provide housing for over 3,000 competitors from around the world. Ronald MacKenzie said the games would be the first "weather-proofed" games unlike the 1932 Olympics because artificial snow making equipment would be installed on Whiteface Mountain for the skiing events. Artificial snow was seven times denser and had proven to hold up better than the real thing.

Support facilities for the Lake Placid organizing committee, the press and the Olympic officials would need to be available along with a broadcast center. The North Elba Town Hall in the center of the village of Lake Placid would be selected for the headquarters of the Lake Placid Olympic Organizing Committee (LPOOC) after it was re-furbished. It was agreed that Lake Placid High School would declare a five week vacation and be transformed into the international press center. The old Lake Placid Club which was called the Lake Placid Resort Hotel would house the IOC and Olympic representatives.

Of course, in addition to building plans for the venues and the planning of the games themselves, the LPOOC would have to handle the logistics of staging the games including hiring a staff, selecting building contractors, preparing for media coverage, raising funding from government and private sources, participating in hearings on the environmental impact and developing a transportation system to move spectators in and out of the area.

From the beginning when Lake Placid was selected in Vienna, there were mixed feelings among local residents. The weekly *Lake Placid News* reported those sentiments on its front page in November 1974 alongside its articles about the triumph of the Vienna selection and the bright economic future the games would bring. Most residents were proud and thrilled about the games coming back to Lake Placid.

The main concern among local residents was that the charming, alpine town they knew might no longer be the same. Though the LPOOC promised a smaller winter games returned to the athlete, these games would be nothing like the quaint competition of 1932. In 1980 there would be 37 nations and over 1300 athletes competing in 37 events. 13,500 people including the athletes would take up residence during the games. Most significantly, there would be 51,000 spectators each day compared with a total of 50,000 for the entire games in 1932. There would be a worldwide television audience of nearly one billion people. There would be over 3000 media representatives in addition to the athletes, coaches and staff members of the national Olympic committees.

Major construction would change the face of the village. There were some who did not welcome the Olympics because of the possible local financial burden. They noted that Lake Placid had only finished paying for the 1932 Olympics in the mid-1960s. They worried what would happen to local taxes after the games and who would maintain all the new facilities. From the beginning, the bid committee and town officials vowed to fight any effort to make the town and taxpayers bear a financial burden or debt. In their minds, Lake Placid was already contributing its infrastructure of many existing facilities which would be renovated and used.

Many in the community felt that change was necessary for economic growth and progress. The *Lake Placid News* editorialized that the village would hold the games "on our terms" and it would be up to the 6000 residents of the town and immediate area to fight to maintain the town's culture and character. These sentiments would continue through the next five and half years and beyond.

For Lake Placid, the Olympics promised an economic boom in a county with a Depression era economy. The unemployment rate in Essex County in the winter was close to 20%. Art Devlin, in boosting the Olympics, told the *Washington Post*,

"From a common sense standpoint, we have to make a living. Our livelihood comes from six weeks a year (the summer tourist season). Our only hope of upgrading the community and not putting smokestacks up or cutting down the trees was the Olympics. The Olympics are something clean and pure. Sports is the only way to put us back on the map. We were dying, badly. We would still be whittling on the street corner," without the Olympics.

It was that economic issue that was central to a debate in the community. There were many who enjoyed the remote, quaint Lake Placid they had always known and they wanted to keep it that way. Devlin's counter argument was that the community would continue to decline and never have an economy to support its people. The Olympics became part of the larger, continuing debate in the Adirondacks between economic development and preserving the environment. Many local residents opposed those they considered elitists - part-time residents wanting to just enjoy the area for recreational and vacation purposes.

There were many others in the community like the North Country boys though who loved winter sports and were just filled with pride for Lake Placid. They wanted the prestige and international recognition of hosting the Olympics one more time in the modern era with all the economic benefits that would bring for the community in the years after.

As the Lake Placid Olympic Organizing Committee (LPOOC) got to work, it realized that its progress was dependent on federal and state funding. Preparing documents and plans and working with state and federal elected officials to get that funding would be a major priority in the early months of planning. Governor Nelson Rockefeller who had been a key supporter of the bid for many years had resigned as Governor at the end of 1973. By 1974 when the Olympic bid was awarded, the Watergate scandal and another scandal had consumed American politics with the President and Vice President both resigning. The fallout led to Rockefeller being called back to public service to serve as Vice President for the new President Gerald R. Ford.

Malcolm Wilson served with Rockefeller as Lt. Governor for all four terms and was Governor in October 1974 when Lake Placid was awarded the games. Just two weeks later though, he was defeated in his own bid for Governor by Congressman Hugh Carey of Brooklyn who took office in January 1975 in the midst of a steep economic downturn. In his first State of the State address, he famously said "the days of wine and roses are over."

Planning for the games had to begin in earnest in 1975. While the bid committee had done extensive research and developed a proposed plan for the Thirteenth Winter Olympics, it would now have to execute the plan. It would have to start by transitioning the bid committee into the Lake Placid Olympic Organizing Committee. The LPOOC, composed mostly of the original bid group, formalized itself as a corporation and Rev. Fell served as the Executive Director. Other community leaders continued to volunteer and serve on various sub-committees that would be responsible for overseeing various plans for the games. Eventually, a small staff was hired.

In 1975 and 1976, the organizing committee had sought to secure funding from the state and federal government and award contracts for management and promotion of the games. Construction would have to begin in two years, by 1977 to be ready for the games. Before that, plans would have to be developed for the new facilities and required public hearings would have to be held about the environmental impact statement. The new construction for the Olympic arena was not questioned. Improvements at the bobsled run and on Whiteface Mountain where the skiing trails would be extended were not controversial.

The LPOOC wanted a Congressional and New York State legislative commitment of funds so they could move ahead. In his 1975-76 supplemental budget proposal, Governor Carey included $1.398 million to provide administrative and support funding for the initial planning period.

Lake Placid would seek $49 million in federal funds which would be used for the construction of the new facilities. This amount was quite a bit higher than the original cost projected in the bid, but New York Congressional leaders said it was better to put in a request for all the funds that might be needed rather than keep returning for additional requests later.

Along with the IOC and the USOC, the State of New York would be the key partner with the LPOOC. In July 1975, Governor Carey officially appointed the New York State Sports Commission which would replace the existing New York State Sports Authority. Secretary of State Mario Cuomo was appointed as Chair along with the Commissioners of the Department of Environmental Conservation, the Department of Parks and Recreation and the Department of Commerce.

Carey set out on an upstate summer tour that included Lake Placid. He signed legislation to create the Commission to plan the state's role in the games. Governor Carey pledged that the Olympics would be "a dividend to our environment, not a detriment."

Roger Tubby, had worked as a press aide to former President Harry Truman and was an active Democratic leader from Plattsburgh. Governor Carey named Tubby to head the Olympic Accommodations Authority which would control housing availability and costs. Tubby was also assigned to be the Governor's personal representative for the games. He attended important meetings and reported any problems or concerns.

At the federal level, Congressman Robert McEwen, who represented the Olympic area, and New York's two Senators, Jacob Javits and James Buckley worked with the Ford Administration agencies and the Congress to secure funding for the games. They worked with the Department of Commerce's Economic Development Agency (EDA) which would administer the Olympic funds. On June 24, 1975, Congressman McEwen introduced a bill authorizing the appropriation of $50 million for construction of facilities. Two days later, Senator Javits and Senator Buckley introduced a similar bill in the Senate.

The LPOOC began meeting and working with environmental groups so that communications were open. They wanted to avoid conflicts like those which evolved in Denver and ended the games there. The New York State Constitution contained a clause saying that the Adirondack Park would be "forever wild," so any proposed developments could not violate the limited conditions for development which were allowed. The Adirondack Park Agency (APA) would be reviewing what would be the biggest and most complex development ever planned for the Adirondacks. The review would have to be thorough but also timely since construction would have to begin as soon as possible.

In November 1975 Governor Carey named Robert Flacke, the town of Lake George Supervisor, to be the Chair of the Adirondack Park Agency. It would be Flacke's responsibility along with Richard Persico, the Executive Director, to oversee the review, balancing the environmental needs with the state's commitment with the LPOOC to hold the Olympics.

Over a five year period, the intent and desire of the North Country boys to run an Olympics "in perspective" would be severely tested. While Lake Placid, unlike Denver had the backing of the state of New York and commitments for federal dollars, the cost of the Olympics would dominate almost all of the preparations. Those preparations would become mired in controversies about cost overruns and financial irregularities, and the impact of construction on the unique "forever wild" Adirondacks.

At the end of 1975, the State of New York and the nation continued to be mired in difficult fiscal times. Newspapers were filled with stories about a possible fiscal collapse and bankruptcy in New York City. Mayor Abe Beame was seeking federal help and the New York *Daily News* ran a famous headline, "Ford to City: Drop Dead." Lake Placid was trying to gain funds and attention in the midst of this city and state crisis. As 1975 ended, the *Lake Placid News* wrote, "Fiscal stringencies, budget cuts and a general pessimistic outlook form a grim outlook for the 1980 Winter Olympics and other programs."

The Bicentennial year dawned with a lot of national enthusiasm. The Innsbruck winter games were just a month away and gave a shot in the arm to the Olympic movement. The Innsbruck games were conducted in a more economical fashion than the Sapporo Olympics. The successful games, which were the first games after the tragedy in Munich in 1972, helped to restore a sense of normalcy and confidence in the Olympics games. With security forces outnumbering athletes by 2 to 1, some felt the security stifled the athletic environment of the games. Americans were thrilled with Dorothy Hamill who became an American sweetheart with her famous hairdo as she won the gold medal in women's figure skating. Six members of the Lake Placid planning group attended to observe the games and by custom, Lake Placid Mayor Robert Peacock was there at the closing ceremonies in Innsbruck to receive the Olympic flag for the next winter games.

The Olympic Games had become very popular in postwar America as live and taped coverage of the Summer and Winter games dominated television for over two weeks back in the 1960s and 1970s when there were still just a handful of television channels. There had only been four Olympic Games held in the United States when Lake Placid was awarded the games. St. Louis hosted the summer games way back in 1904. Both Lake Placid and Los Angeles hosted the games in 1932 and then Squaw Valley, California hosted the Winter Olympics in 1960 in the black and white television era. The Lake Placid Olympics would be the first held in the United States in a newer era of color television and when a whole generation of Baby Boomers had become adults.

Televised coverage of the Olympics had come a long way from the black and white coverage in Squaw Valley twenty years earlier. CBS had bid $50,000 to televise those games. As the winter and summer games moved to Europe and Japan in 1964, new satellites and underwater cables offered new opportunities for live broadcasts of some events and tape delayed coverage. Before the satellites at the Rome Summer Olympics in 1960, ABC took film and sent it to New York on an airplane every night. Four years later in Innsbruck, ABC paid $500,000 for the rights to televise the games. However, it still sent the videotapes to Paris and flew them to New York for showing. For the first time though, the opening ceremonies had been shown live via satellite.

ABC paid $2 million for the 1968 games in Grenoble, France and finally had same night taped coverage and the first live coverage of a sports event outside the United States. NBC finally beat out ABC and paid $6 million to televise the 1972 games in Sapporo, Japan. NBC's coverage was panned and four years later, ABC won the rights again in Innsbruck for the meager price of $10 million.

Twenty years after Squaw Valley, the winter games were coming back to the United States. This would be the first time most Americans had color television to watch live coverage in Eastern Standard Time from Lake Placid. At Innsbruck, private discussions were held by Lake Placid officials with ABC Sports executives about the broadcasting rights to the Lake Placid games. In those days, the IOC did not take the lead in awarding broadcasting rights. Lake Placid officials made a tentative agreement with ABC which set off a testy controversy between IOC Director,

Mme. Monique Berlioux and John Wilkins, head of the LPOOC Broadcasting and Marketing Committee.

Mme Berlioux was a tough woman totally committed to the Olympic movement and was called "the most powerful woman in sports." She served as the right hand to IOC Chairman Lord Killanin. She was a valuable source of support and technical help to Olympic organizing committees and she visited Lake Placid as it was making its preparations for the games.

She had been a French national swimming champion and an Olympian herself on the 1948 French swim team when she famously would not let an appendectomy three weeks before the games stop her from swimming. She grew up in Nazi-occupied France during World War II and helped the resistance by swimming the Seine to deliver messages. She even threw her shoes at a German soldier after he jumped in a pool on top of her.

Lake Placid needed money and it wanted to cut a deal with ABC as soon as it could. The IOC had advised Lake Placid to not negotiate any deals until after the Innsbruck games, thinking the value of the contract would be higher. ABC, NBC and CBS had all expressed interest in televising the games after they were awarded to Lake Placid. However, only ABC's Roone Arledge had maintained contact after conducting a feasibility study. There had been no follow up from NBC and CBS. Defying the wishes of the IOC, the LPOOC and ABC made an agreement which included a $250,000 advance to Lake Placid that would be refundable if the contract was not finalized by the IOC.

After the Innsbruck Olympics, NBC and CBS became more interested and wanted a piece of the action. They complained about the secrecy of the LPOOC-ABC agreement. The IOC refused to approve the contract with ABC which forced a re-consideration and a bidding process. Both networks were given a chance to bid. Jack Wilkins, the chair of the LPOOC Broadcasting and Marketing

Committee, sought a meeting with Berlioux but she rebuffed him, saying "I am afraid that at the moment, I work for the IOC and am not under orders from the LPOOC." ABC was the low bidder but had the opportunity to outbid the other two and won the rights to broadcast the games for $15.5 million.

Another nuisance to the planning occurred when State Assemblyman Larry Lane of Greene County introduced a bill to move the skating events to Albany and build a new arena there. Nothing came of it.

In April 1976, the LPOOC held a public meeting to discuss plans and progress and to solicit questions from residents. A major concern of residents was how transportation would be addressed and to make sure they were still able to move around town and get to the grocery store. Already, because of the limit on the number of visitors, there were thoughts about using a bus system with peripheral parking lots in outlying areas which would restrict the number of cars entering the area where the games would be held.

While the LPOOC was pursuing state and federal funding for the new and renovated sports facilities, it still had to find some funding to construct an athletes village to house competitors. Federal funding required that all facilities built had to have a plan for after-use. In May, Congressman McEwen noted that, in addition to federal funds for construction of the sports venues, there might be a good opportunity to get federal funding from the Bureau of Prisons for the athletes village if Camp Adirondack could be converted into a federal prison. Governor Carey asked Secretary of State Cuomo to figure out what to do with Camp Adirondack, a juvenile detention facility that the state was closing. There had been some talk that the facility could be the location for the Olympic athletes' village.

Lake Placid still did not have much money to operate in the spring of 1976. Senators Buckley and Javits and Congressman

McEwen had tried to get an early commitment from President Ford so that it could report that to the IOC at its meeting at the Innsbruck games. While the Lake Placid committee and its progress report were well received in Innsbruck, IOC officials were concerned. Jack Shea reported, "The one question they asked at the IOC meeting was, 'Would federal financing be forthcoming?' We said yes."

The IOC was not satisfied though with letters of encouragement from President Ford and Lord Killanin said the IOC would be asking for detailed answers at its next meeting in Montreal during the summer games. Jack Shea added, "When they look at us, they have Denver and Salt Lake City on their minds." Also in Montreal that summer, the IOC officials meeting there would question the Lake Placid representatives about the viability of the transportation plan being considered.

On May 7, 1976 President Ford hosted American Olympic winners from Innsbruck at the White House as well as members of the LPOOC. Ronald MacKenzie presented the President, an avid skier, with a giant ticket to the games and invited him to be the first to ski down the Olympic course at Whiteface. The President indicated that it was his intention to attend the games in 1980, assuming he would win the election and still be in the White House, but only as a spectator. Emphasizing his commitment to amateur sports, he also announced his proposal for $28 million for construction of facilities for the games were an investment in new permanent facilities for training of American athletes. His proposed funding was less than the LPOOC sought but that would be negotiated as it made its way through Congress. A $49 million bill was finally passed and signed by President Ford on September 29, 1976.

New York City, New York State and the federal government were facing severe economic problems in the mid 1970's and providing state funds for the Olympics was questioned by some. The United States had already experienced a lack of financial appetite for it in Denver and Salt Lake City. *New York Times* Sports Editor Jack Murphy wrote in 1976, after the successful conclusion of the 1976 games in Innsbruck, "How can Congress appropriate $50 million for the winter games in Lake Placid when the City of New York is on the edge of bankruptcy? Will the Winter Olympics survive? Do they deserve to survive? Reluctantly, I must say no."

In July the summer games, which took place in Montreal, just two hours from Lake Placid, were held without incident. Canada hosted a grand but costly debt-ridden spectacle that was highlighted by the gymnastic gold medal performances of Romania's fourteen-year-old gymnast Nadia Comeneci. However, the games were left with the legacy of a massive debt. The province of Quebec and the government of Canada had not only a debt of $1.6 billion but also incomplete facilities. Montreal Mayor Jean Drapeau would be continually haunted by his statement that, "The Montreal Olympics can no more have a deficit, than a man can have a baby."

The Montreal committee had called their Olympics a games "in moderation," in contrast to the expensive games in the years before. By the time the games were over, the Olympic Stadium was referred as the "Big O" and then derisively as the "Big Owe." The debt was not paid for 30 years by the citizens of Quebec until 2006. The stadium was never completely finished for the 1976 games and then, on two occasions in the 1990s when it was home to the Montreal Expos baseball team, two large sections of it collapsed. Now, it sits without a sports tenant and is a monument to impractical Olympic planning and expense.

In the second half of 1976, some funding came to Lake Placid. A technical assistance grant from the Economic Development Administration of the US Department of Commerce enabled the LPOOC to hire Greg McConnell as Director of Program Planning in October 1976. Since the LPOOC members were focused on the finances and construction, McConnell and two other staff were to be the professional arm of the organization to focus on many of the details of operating the games. They were operating without a lot of cash because they waited for Congress and New York State to fund administration costs and construction.

An Environmental Impact Statement (EIS) was required before any of the $49 million of federal money approved by Congress could be spent on the Olympics. The voluminous study, over six inches thick, was done by Sasaki Associates of Watertown, Massachusetts. It received a positive review from new DEC Commissioner Peter Berle who had replaced Ogden Reid. It reported positive economic benefits for the area and a growth in tourism and long term employment. The EIS determined that a limit of 51,000 spectators would be all the area could handle every day so planning for the games proceeded with that limit.

Chapter Four

The Environmental Challenge

"No jumps, no games, no games, no Lake Placid."

—Art Devlin, quoted in the *Washington Post*

In the fall of 1976, despite the initial cooperative relationship, some skirmishing began between the LPOOC and environmentalists. Hearings were held in November 1976 in Albany by the United States Department of Commerce's Economic Development Administration.

The proposed 90 meter ski jump, rising 266 feet at Intervale, two miles west of the village of Lake Placid was addressed in the statement. A negative aspect of the ski jump tower would be the "visual impact" of the view from John Brown's farm, a state historic site. John Brown, the abolitionist, was buried there in December 1859 after he was killed in an insurrection against slavery in Harpers Ferry, West Virginia. He had set up the farm as a place for African American slaves to move who were fleeing the South. Ronald McKenzie, President of the LPOOC offered a different view, saying that the ski jump complex would lead to more tourism including to the John Brown farm.

The construction of the two new ski jump towers drew the criticism of the Sierra Club and other environmentalists who decided to intervene in public hearings. The Sierra Club viewed the proposed ski jumps at Intervale as a blight on the mountain scenery that would be forever scarred, destroying the beauty and wilderness of the Adirondack region. It was like a "the visual equivalent of putting an illuminated 26 story apartment building" in the mountains, said James Dumont of the Sierra Club. The Sierra Club also said the Olympics would produce new motels and shops "with neon sign after neon sign" and criticized the lack of detailed transportation plan. Many felt the environmental protests and threats were real and damaging.

Some environmentalists were interested in changing the sites and venues for the different sports, according to Robert Flacke who was the chair of the Adirondack Park Agency (APA). He said some of the groups were interested in holding events all across the North Country rather than holding them all in the High Peaks area which required road re-building and other construction destroying many acres of wilderness.

The Sierra Club questioned the widening of the two lane roads leading to Lake Placid through the Cascade Pass on Route 73 from Keene, saying that 1000 trees in the forested areas would be cut down. The Sierra Club later went to court and received an injunction against the road project until the state could prove it had done an environmental impact study. Eventually the injunction was lifted when the state submitted a report on its deliberations and the road construction went ahead.

After the first hearing on the Environmental Impact Study in Lake Placid on November 10, the media gave extensive coverage to the environmentalists' challenges. According to a *Lake Placid News* report, the first hearing "shocked supporters of the games to the stark realization that the 1980 event could be in jeopardy." Members of the LPOOC and their political supporters were alarmed and mobilized to make sure they were well represented when the next hearing took place in late November at the Legislative Office Building in Albany.

Leaders from construction unions including former US Labor Secretary Peter Brennan testified in support of the games. Brennan said, "If we lose them (the games) we look like a bunch of jerks." Local officials made sure to testify in force at the hearing in Albany and they attacked the Sierra Club. Vernon Lamb, chair of the LPOOC environmental council said, "It has been the choice of the Sierra Club to abandon the role of a credible and responsible environmental organization. With no basis in fact, they have deliberately resorted to unfounded, distorted and incorrect public statements."

The aggressive stance of the Sierra Club led to a split with the Adirondack Council and the Adirondack Mountain Club, which preferred a more cooperative approach to planning and working with the LPOOC. Courtney Jones, Chair of the Adirondack Council told *Sports Illustrated*, "To oppose the Olympics for their own sake would be the height of irresponsibility. We simply want to be certain that all the questions are asked and all the issues tested."

Those who had followed the events in Denver began to wonder whether the environmental movement, which had helped derail the Denver games, might threaten Lake Placid's plans. Greg McConnell said, "You came every day wondering if this was going to be your last week at work." However, the Sierra Club said they were not interested in scuttling the games, just challenging the plans. The environmental controversy led by the Sierra Club even made some in the International Olympic Committee unnerved after the experience in Denver. Jack Shea said that two members of the IOC had questioned him whether the games in Lake Placid were threatened by environmentalists.

Department of Environmental Conservation Commissioner Peter Berle told the *New York Times* on December 30, 1976, "I'm not impressed by those suggesting the Olympics may be shifted to a foreign country because of discussions now in progress with environmentalists." He stated that the public hearings and debate were part of the process of approval for spending state and federal taxpayer dollars earmarked for the games.

The decision on the ski jumps would be made by the Adirondack Park Agency headed by Flacke. The APA was only three years old in 1976 and it had already become controversial to local residents who viewed it as the heavy head of government regulating local land use on private property and threatening the ability for the local economy to grow. It had been established by Governor Nelson Rockefeller and the State Legislature primarily to regulate land use on private properties in the Adirondack Park. Much of the land was public but the APA's mission was to preserve the park and regulate development. Local residents were so incensed they began an effort in the State Legislature to repeal the agency.

Flacke turned the ski jump issue over to a hearing officer, Victor Yannacone, who sought to keep the decision-making time frame on track. The APA was set to vote on the ski jumps and other plans in early January 1977. This was a crucial vote and some felt the decision would determine the fate of the Olympics as time was ticking with only three years until the start of the games. Any further delays would threaten the construction timetable. An alternate site for the ski jumps was being proposed in the town of Jay on land owned by the state. Some were pushing for that alternative but the LPOOC leaders were not supportive. Rev. Fell and others said they would not go to the IOC to change the location because they did not trust the Department of Environmental Conservation. He and others felt that the alternate site did not have much detail and it would take months it get it studied and approved.

Governor Carey's chief of staff, Robert Morgado, called Flacke and said the Governor was anxious for the permit to get approved. Flacke assured him, "as Chairman, I counted my votes." He knew there were enough for passage. On January 8 1977, the vote to approve the ski jumps at Intervale was approved by the APA. Robert Flacke explained his vote in favor saying that to delay the vote was "merely a ploy." He said that he had to weigh the visual impact of the ski jump towers and the potential advantages for the Olympics and he said the balance clearly favored the Intervale site.

The Sierra Club was disappointed but did not want to sue the committee. Samuel Sage of the Sierra Club said "We don't want the International Olympic Committee to think we are trying to delay the games."

By April 1977, the Sierra Club re-affirmed that it was not going to court. It had reached an agreement with Secretary of State Mario Cuomo and other state officials that would meet its major objectives in order to protect the environment. This included overuse of wilderness areas, highway expansion projects and the APA's process for reviewing and approving the ski jumps.

Finally, on April 21, 1977, the official Ground Breaking Ceremony was held for the new facilities which would have to be built in less than three years. The Gilbane Construction Company was chosen as the general contractor to oversee all the construction projects for the LPOOC. Businesses and schools were closed and six area high school bands participated in a parade to mark the event. ABC's Jim McKay was the Master of Ceremonies and speakers included Ronald MacKenzie along with Congressman Robert McEwen, and State Senator Robert Stafford. New York State Environmental Conservation Commissioner Peter Berle said, "I am committed to an environmentally-sound Olympics which will contribute to a healthy economy in Lake Placid. There is no question that this can be done and I am going to see that's it's made to happen."

Also attending and speaking were a son and daughter of Governor Carey and Chip Carter, son of President Jimmy Carter. He would man a diesel shovel to scoop the first bite of earth for the new arena. He said he expected his father to attend and open the games in 1980.

In July 1977, the State Legislature approved and Governor Carey signed a bill to authorize a special Olympic lottery which had a goal of providing a $100 million trust fund to maintain the facilities after the games. The bill passed the Assembly 115-23 but some dissented including Assemblyman Charles Schumer who complained about the "rah'rah commitment to Olympics, Olympics, Olympics when we have much more pressing problems to deal with."

New York State would provide over $40 million for the games with $32 million for capital costs and over $10 million for operating costs and security. There were also countless hours of many employees in the fourteen state agencies which were involved in assisting the Olympic effort. In addition to the APA, and the DEC the Department of Labor handled over 4000 placements for jobs for the games.

As construction started, it produced a dramatic improvement in the local economy with a new Hilton Hotel and expansions at the Mirror Lake Inn, the Holiday Inn and other hotels. During the first thirteen months of construction, the unemployment rate in Essex County dropped ten percentage points from 17 percent to 7.1 percent. It fell 6.4 percent in Franklin County and 5.3 percent in Clinton County. 82.6 percent of the construction workers were from within a 90 mile radius of Lake Placid. Olympic related construction employment rose from 30 to 400 from May to December 1977.

Governor Carey returned to Lake Placid on a hot day in late August 1977 to see the progress on building the facilities and venues. He made a stop at the new ski jump construction site and was asked if he would take a turn on it. With his Irish wit, he replied, "First, I will let Mr. Duryea and Mr. Anderson (the

Republicans legislative leaders) try a jump and I'll make my judgment after they land." Carey said he would like to return for the opening of the games in 1980 as Governor, not a spectator, a reference to his hope to be re-elected in 1978.

Meanwhile, Carey had surprisingly announced in February that New York City would begin considering a bid for the 1984 summer games. With costs mushrooming, only American cities would be seriously bidding. Los Angeles was the favored major contender but Boston, Chicago, New Orleans and Atlanta were also planning to formally express interest. Tehran, Iran had planned to bid but withdrew.

The New York City bid was scoffed at by the media and other critics, given the costs, but Carey asked for $400,000 for a feasibility study in a supplemental budget request to the Legislature. He appointed a close ally, Richard Ravitch, former head of the Urban Development Corporation, to coordinate the initial planning.

Ravitch's report concluded that New York City would lose over $250 billion on the summer games but Carey suggested that the state would cover those costs through the state lottery proceeds and other state funds.

Promoting Los Angeles' bid against New York, California Governor Jerry Brown raised the specter of crime in New York City in the midst of the summer of the Son of Sam on the loose. Governor Carey said he resented that and said that Los Angeles had its own legacy of crime with the Manson family. Los Angeles had an advantage going in since it was chosen as the US bidder for the 1976 and 1980 summer games and had already prepared plans many years earlier for those past bids. New York's effort was put together in a short time. On September 25, the USOC chose Los Angeles over New York by a margin of 55-39.

Chapter Five

The Olympic Prison

"How can the Carter Administration with its campaign for human rights, turn a symbol of international harmony in Lake Placid into a prison for Blacks and Hispanics from our urban ghettoes?"

—Brian Wilson, a leader of Stop the Olympic Prison (STOP)

I n addition to building and renovating the sports venues, the LPOOC focused on building the athletes village to house participants from all over the world. Security at the village was a paramount concern after the slaying of Israeli athletes in the Olympic village in Munich in 1972. The federal funds for the games were available on the condition that the facilities would have an afteruse. Those funds would pay for new sports facilities but not for athlete housing in an Olympic village.

Congressman McEwen also learned that additional federal money from the Bureau of Prisons could be available to construct the athletes' village and living quarters if they were converted to a medium security prison after the games. The idea of a prison in the Adirondacks was appealing to the Bureau. It had been wanting to build another federal prison in the Northeast but had run into opposition in many communities. Building a housing complex for the Olympics had similar security needs as a prison. Plans for the athletes' village/prison received federal approval in January 1977. The whole complex was several miles outside of Lake Placid in Ray Brook between Lake Placid and Saranac Lake to the west. It would be surrounded by barbed wire and heavy security.

brochure from STOP coalition

The proposal was underway without the usual public hearings and the decision of the LPOOC to pursue this option became one of the biggest controversies in the years leading up to the games. It ran right into a wall of opposition from an active criminal justice movement that was trying to reform public policies and stop the expansion of incarceration rather than alternative means of punishment and rehabilitation.

Religious groups were in the vanguard against the building of new prisons. When activists learned of the Olympic prison proposal, they quickly mobilized and on March 22, 1977 formed an organization called STOP (Stop the Olympic Prison) which was housed at the offices of the New York State Council of Churches in Syracuse. It was also sponsored by the National Moratorium on Prison Construction.

The Coalition was particularly opposed to prison facilities in remote locations far away from the family members of those incarcerated. Civil rights groups also opposed building a prison for mostly inner city convicts in a remote region of the state. While terrorism was a concern for the Olympic committee, opponents of the prison raised the specter of American history repeating itself right in New York State. They cited the 1971 uprising of minority downstate prisoners far away at Attica State Prison near Buffalo which ended with 39 prisoners and guards dead.

Religious activists around the nation and soon, around the world learned that the United States was planning to house Olympic athletes in rooms that would be constructed to become prison cells. The uproar that followed reached all the way to Washington and to the Olympic committees in other countries. Protests were held outside United States embassies in London and the Hague, Netherlands. The issue became fodder for national and international politics as it was being considered at the same time as President Jimmy Carter came into the White House with human rights as the centerpiece of his foreign policy. He criticized the treatment of political dissidents by autocratic government around the world, whether they were Communist or right wing military dictatorships. He said positive American foreign relations with those countries would be directly related to their human rights records.

Opponents asked what the United States would be saying if the Soviet Union was proposing to turn the athletes' village for the Moscow summer games into a prison. STOP even discussed whether to urge a boycott of the Lake Placid games unless the prison plan was changed.

The opposition continued to spread and became a cause celebre among national religious organizations and civil rights leaders. Vernon Jordan, President of the National Urban League, said, "It is our view that such use of the buildings would make a hollow mockery of the purposes of the Olympics and greatly embarrass the United States." Rev. Jon Regier, Executive Director of the New York State Conference of Churches had worked with civil rights leader Andrew Young in the 1960s. He sent a letter to Young, then the US ambassador to the United Nations, asking him to intercede and have President Carter to halt the plan.

However, there was a different feeling in the North Country. Most welcomed not only the federal funds which would benefit the Olympics but the 200 permanent jobs at the prison that would be created after the games concluded were very welcome to many in a region with chronic unemployment. The *Adirondack Daily Enterprise* editorialized, "The area has always taken the unwanted, beginning with the tubercular, then drug addicts, now the men at the state's Camp Adirondack."

The Saranac Lake Clergy Association and the Lake Placid Clergy Association parted with their activist brethren from downstate and the rest of the country when they issued a statement supporting the prison. They acknowledged the difficulty of criminal justice issues and the need for reform but they directly attacked the rhetoric and characterizations of those opposing the prison,

"Prison opposition rhetoric has not been kind to our area and its people. We object to the characterizations being presented. Our remoteness is certainly being overstated. We are in New York State, not deepest Siberia. If all things must be measured by distance from New York City, we are closer than currently existing federal facilities for young convicted felons. A much worse characterization being given in the opposition rhetoric to the Ray Brook facility is that our people are igno-

rant and prejudiced whites who are to be placed as "the herdsmen of the minorities' constituting the prison population."

Ten other clergy in Essex and Franklin counties didn't agree with this sentiment and issued their own letter to show that not all religious leaders in the region favored the plan. Even though it was in the middle of the controversy, the LPOOC did not feel it was the target of the protest which they viewed more as a political argument between the protesters and the federal government over the after-use of the facility.

The STOP activists started pressuring Congress to stop funding for the prison. Forty persons protested outside the White House gates in December 1978. STOP was not opposed to the Olympics just the prison and they pushed what seemed a logical alternative. Rather than a prison, they wanted the athletes' village to be turned into housing for one of the permanent US Olympic training sites which were then being considered.

The *New York Times* editorialized against the prison in January 1979, and supported the advocates' alternative, saying, "There are preferable sites in or near New York City." It further suggested that Lake Placid's athletes' village would be better as the permanent winter sports training facility which the USOC wanted.

STOP also produced a dramatic poster with a hand holding an Olympic torch behind a prison bar and the Olympic rings. This went too far for the US Olympic Committee. In August 1978, Don Miller, Executive Director of the USOC wrote a letter to STOP saying, "the USOC requests that you immediately cease and desist from using the world 'Olympic' as well as utilization of the Olympic rings on any material under your control...Rest assured this office will take all steps that are necessary to insure compliance with the law."

Michael Kroll, a coordinator with STOP, said the organization would not do as Miller asked, "Our poster is not for profit but for political action. As such it falls squarely within the First Amendment. "

With legal representation from the American Civil Liberties Union, STOP sued the USOC and won a court ruling, asserting that the protection given to the Olympics symbols only extended to commercial uses, not to public issues. The court cited a case, Spence v. Washington which involved the American flag as a symbol like the Olympic rings. "The Supreme Court held that a college student's public display of an upside-down American flag, to which he had affixed a peace symbol, was a form of expression protected by the first amendment, the court stated (in that case), "there was no risk that appellant's acts would mislead viewers into assuming that the Government endorsed his viewpoint. To the contrary, he was plainly and peacefully protesting the fact that it did not'. Accordingly, since the defendant (the USOC) has failed to prove its counterclaims, they are dismissed. The plaintiff is entitled to a Judgment declaring that its poster does not violate section 380 of Title 36, United States Code, or infringe any of the defendant's trademark rights."

Meanwhile artist Amy Schneider's cute Olympic poster of Roni, Lake Placid's Raccoon mascot, grabbing the Olympic rings had to be recalled because, according to Olympic rules, the rings cannot be touched. The LPOOC compensated her for the cost of her posters. The *New Yorker* magazine noted that the IOC "did grudgingly permit the Religious Affairs Committee of the LPOOC to issue a poster on which some thin heavenly rays nicked a couple of the rings."

Despite the controversy, the construction began on the prison complex and the protest effort would continue in its effort to change the afteruse of the athletes village.

Chapter Six

Rumors, Suspicions, Doubts

"We were in shock at the realities of putting on the games and dealing with governmental authorities regarding funding, environmental regulations, transportation and so much more."

—Rev. Bernard Fell, Executive Director,
Lake Placid Olympic Organizing Committee

As 1978 dawned the games were just two years away and all around the village, the progress toward that goal was becoming more visible. One of the requirements for the Olympics was that the venues had to stage a world competition prior to the games to test them. The first venue for competition that was completed was the 400 meter speed skating oval in front of Lake Placid High School, though construction had been briefly stopped. The Department of Environmental Conservation determined that a coolant being used for the underground refrigeration was toxic but a substitute was then used.

Fifty seven skaters from 15 nations took part in the 1978 World Championship games at Lake Placid. 8000 persons attended skating events along with world bobsledding competitions being held at the Winter Sports Festival weekend sponsored by New

York State. Lake Placid's new oval would be one of the last of an Olympic era with speed skating competition held outdoors. New indoor speed skating facilities would be constructed for all the games after Sarajevo in 1984.

The only other refrigerated 400 meter oval in the country was in West Allis, Wisconsin. Not coincidentally, that was where the men's overall world champion speed skater resided. 19-year-old Eric Heiden came to Lake Placid with his sister, Beth, to race in the world championships on the new oval. He wrote years later about his beginning as a skater in the *New York Times*, "At age 14, I was committed to the sport, and the next seven years revolved around speed skating, I simply wanted to skate as fast I could."

At age 17 he skated on the US team in Innsbruck and finished seventh in one race. At age 19, he was already considered a golden boy of skating. In Lake Placid that winter, he proved he was the favorite to win the Olympics when he blazed along the new oval to easily win the overall men's title for the second consecutive year. The year before he had won it in the Netherlands and became the first American to do so in the 76 year history of the competition. Beth Heiden finished second in the Lake Placid competition. In the junior world championships in Montreal in 1978, Eric and Beth swept all four races, the first time any skaters had done that.

Lord Killanin came from Ireland to Lake Placid with several other IOC members to watch the world championships at the new venues and was pleased with what he saw. "I am leaving with complete confidence that the 1980 Olympic Winter Games will be very successful. Gentlemen, I would say that you have conquered your greatest problems. You have made far more progress than anyone could have expected."

Despite the successful conduct of the international world competitions, Killanin's public expression of confidence was not shared by Governor Carey and top state leaders who were responsible for approving funds for the games and assisting Lake Placid in preparations and management. Chuck Carlson of the state Department of Transportation had been "loaned" to provide professional support for the LPOOC. However, a sense of serious concern was beginning to grip top state leaders as they worked with and watched the LPOOC become mired in controversies about their use of public and private funding.

Tens of millions of dollars would be spent on the Lake Placid games and yet the management of the games was still in the hands of a small staff and volunteers who had had never run an international event of this magnitude. Rumors and questions circulated about the use of state money by the LPOOC. Many members of the community were also becoming suspicious and even disgusted about perceived high salaries and contracts that were awarded to local businesses, some of which were connected with members of the committee.

Committee members responded that it was a small town and many of them had their own businesses. They said it was impossible to award local contracts and make logistical decisions that would be without benefit to anyone affiliated with the games. Rev. Fell told the *Boston Globe*, "When we testified before the [Congressional] committee that was one of the things that we alluded to with great pride. That we had husbands and wives and sons and daughters all involved. We are proud of our nepotism up in the country. We need our relatives. The Lord knows there are a lot of them and we are proud of it."

Residents of Lake Placid who rented apartments found themselves evicted so landlords could rent their properties for much higher amounts for the month of the Olympics, or even for a few weeks. Rental fees averaged $15,000 for the month with high end homes getting $40,000. The renters formed a group called RACCOONS, Renters Association of Concerned Citizens on Ousting Our Needed Services. Among them were many service workers such as bartenders, clerks, waitresses and chambermaids.

The disputes over the ski jumps had been resolved and the prison controversy would continue with protests all the way to the games in 1980. In 1978, these other controversies, which had been building, began to expose deep divisions in the town as some residents resented what they viewed as the greed of some business leaders and landlords.

Rev. William Hayes from St. Eustace Church on Main Street said, "Everyone's trying to get their share of the dollar and some people are trying to get their share of the dollar at the expense of their neighbors...It's as if there has been an oil strike nearby or legalized gambling has been introduced," he commented to *Sports Illustrated*.

Governor Hugh Carey and his staff realized that there were many state agencies involved in supporting the Olympics and that there needed to be some central authority regarding spending and budgeting of state resources.

Robert Flacke said the state was becoming so concerned about the financial affairs and wasteful spending of the LPOOC that Governor Carey decided to put him in charge of all state spending for the games. Quoting Governor Carey, Flacke said the Governor called a meeting and said "if you are going to spend a nickel you have to have his [Flacke's] signature."

State Budget Director Red Miller issued a memorandum advising agency heads that they would now be working through Flacke as the state's liaison for finance with the LPOOC. Mark Lawton, the deputy budget director, said that Governor Carey was "very opinionated but very honest. The only thing he asked of you was competence and no personal agenda." Lawton said the Governor told him that "funny stuff is going on" and "I do not want any state employee going to jail" over activities associated with the Olympics.

Lawton said the Governor and his staff also decided the LPOOC needed help. Carey and his staff felt a seasoned professional who had managed large scale events needed to be hired as the general manager to pull things together in the critical year and a half remaining before the games began.

However, the LPOOC had a strong desire to maintain local control. Committee members felt they had been bidding and studying the Olympics for years and they wanted to maintain their control over the games. Lawton said that he and Governor Carey tried to respect the desire for local control and that they were sensitive to the fact that the Adirondacks was a Republican-controlled area. Lawton said the Governor's office often solicited the opinions and support of Republican Senate Majority Leader Warren Anderson and other upstate senators on Olympic issues.

Being in charge of the state's finances, Miller, Lawton and the budget division insisted that no state funds would be spent without a plan and government accountability. In light of many news stories reporting questionable expenses and contracting with relatives and friends, they did not have confidence that the local committee had the management expertise to pull the games together. Lawton said the LPOOC needed outside help because committee leaders had no idea how to negotiate contracts and organize the Olympics. "They were still mired in 1932, running it like it was a church chicken barbeque."

Governor Carey and his staff asked the General Electric Company for recommendations of a few people who could handle the job of overseeing the Olympics and making it a success. By holding the purse strings, they had the power to insist on having a manager to oversee the preparations throughout the critical final year and a half of preparations. Only one name came back from General Electric's leadership and it was Petr Spurney. According to Lawton and Flacke, they insisted that the LPOOC hire Spurney. Flacke said he told Fell and MacKenzie that "if they didn't hire Spurney the state would have to re-think its investment,"

which included not only funding but the assignment of many
state agency employees to help with the games.

The LPOOC voted to hire Spurney though many members of
the committee felt they didn't need outside help. One of the
members though, Serge Lussi, was very worried about whether
the LPOOC could pull off the games. He felt the committee was
in great need of a person with business experience to manage the
games. "We have nobody here to run this," he told the members. The committee finally voted 28-4 to hire Spurney. "Once
he came in, I didn't worry about anything," Lussi said.

Spurney went to Lake Placid to meet with local leaders but he
was not sure he wanted to take the job. If it was just the Lake
Placid people, he probably would not have taken the job. Spurney said a member of the committee said they were looking for a
"bus driver," someone to drive the bus that was already on the
road. Spurney was not looking just to drive the bus but felt they
needed him to take charge of the whole event. Spurney said the
LPOOC thought it was their show and they did not want to give
authority to someone else to be making decisions.

"I would not have come without the state's commitment," Spurney said. State officials told him they would provide the support
he needed to do the job. He said his appointment represented
kind of a "tipping point," when everyone involved realized they
all had to buckle down and pull together as a team with a leader
in the final sixteen months to successfully pull the games off.

Petr Spurney had earned a record as an efficient manager of
"mega-events." He had a background in mechanical engineering
and had a successful career in international marketing selling air-
planes. He had successfully turned around the Spokane Expo in
1974 and put it in the black. Spurney had also managed the
Bicentennial American Freedom Train, which traveled the country in 1975-1976 with artifacts of American history. At Lake
Placid, he was hired for $100,000 and would serve as general

manager to oversee the entire operations of the games for the remaining year and a half. He also had a bonus clause in his contract giving him a percentage of savings up to $50,000 for reducing costs. Within a few months, Spurney said he had already cut costs by several million dollars.

Spurney would get his baptism by fire as controversies about the preparations for the games began to swirl in local gossip and in the media. He had to immediately address a marketing lawsuit from two firms who said their contracts had been broken by illegal actions when the LPOOC took money out of escrow accounts. Also, the United States Postal Service revoked the committee's discount rate on the grounds it made a mistake in granting it based on "educational purposes," which they felt was not the case. Spurney and the LPOOC would also have to respond to an audit by the federal Department of Commerce, which became concerned about questionable contracts and other financial issues

Like all the Olympics before, the cost of the Lake Placid games, though modest in comparison, rose and exceeded its budget by over $14 million. Spurney and Rev. Fell were forced to go back to Albany and Washington to seek additional money to complete preparations for the games. They were given assurances from New York State that the money would be there while the federal government was more hesitant to commit any more funds.

The *Lake Placid News* wrote on Spurney's arrival, "Few envy Petr J. Spurney, his $100,000-a-year job as general manager of the LPOOC. Hardly had he been named by a 28 to 4 vote of the committee then the roof caved in."

Spurney would say that running the Olympics was like "a war with no shooting," because he had to manage so many fronts all at once: the finances, facilities construction, marketing, international relations, dealings with all the sports federations, working with the LPOOC plus public relations and other administration.

Spurney's view was that the original Lake Placid committee that won the Olympic bid got the "goose with the golden egg" but they didn't know how to then pull off the games. "They knew their winter sports - they knew the community of athletes," he noted but like other Olympic committees they needed professional leadership to run the games. Spurney had the experience and viewed that running such events is a threefold operation: planning, implementation and dissolution.

LPOOC General Manager Petr Spurney with Lake Placid Mayor Robert Peacock (Lake Placid Olympic Museum photo)

Spurney said his charge was to break even and pay all the bills. He was also focused on having room for 13,000 who needed to run the games, counting national Olympic committees, athletes, the media, security, LPOOC employees and others.

Many local business people in Lake Placid felt that there was not enough help from Spurney and the LPOOC in planning how they would handle 51,000 people every day who had to be fed and find toilet facilities.

Spurney said, "We are building an Olympics for the athlete. There will be some spectators but to 600 million people it is an event that will be viewed through television."

Many people in the community resented what they felt was Spurney's no nonsense, take charge, bottom-line way of doing business. They thought he was heavy-handed. That was a sentiment shared by many members of the LPOOC according to Jim Rogers, the former local radio station owner who served as Protocol Committee chair. However, the Lake Placid committee, which had been comprised of neighbors and friends and relatives, was not always willing to trust outside experts when they had to be involved with overseeing what they were doing. They felt that way not just about Spurney, but also about their old adversary, the State of New York, which was also trying to maintain fiscal accountability. The federal government with its audit underway was also viewed as adversarial as it pored over the expenses being charged to the federal funds.

Spurney felt the local antipathy, especially since he was an outsider brought in to take control over what the locals felt was theirs. He noted, "Lake Placid is a very difficult place to live much less work unless you have those roots."

William Kissel, who was chief counsel for the LPOOC, felt that Spurney did a tremendous job to resolve problems and manage things with the federal and state governments in order to have the games ready. "They [the organizing committee] very well needed him," Kissel asserted. Greg McConnell, who worked for Spurney also supported him, said, "He didn't tell them what they wanted to hear, he told them what they should hear."

Rev. Fell and other members of the committee were upset with all the negative media coverage of the planning for the games. He felt there had not been enough positive press about how a small town had managed to pull together the Olympic Games when many larger communities could not.

Rev. William Hayes, rector of St. Eustace Episcopal Church on Main Street in Lake Placid told the *Watertown Daily Times*, "When the Olympics are over, there'll be a tremendous emotional letdown while people put their lives back together and rearrange themselves in whatever degree they were disrupted. But I believe it will take a long time to heal the wounds that have been opened by local against local person. We don't forget up here. I still hear it from 1932."

Planning was underway in Los Angeles for the 1984 summer games and things were not going great there either. By 1978, Rev. Fell had become so frustrated about the problems and the negative publicity, he would tell a Los Angeles Olympics staff person for the 1984 Summer Games to "give em back," when asked what advice he would offer. Many local residents were also tired of controversy and worried about the reputation of Lake Placid.

While Lake Placid was having its problems, Los Angeles was at an impasse with the IOC about financial responsibility for the 1984 summer games. After the huge deficit in Montreal two years earlier, the city of Los Angeles did not want to commit to that responsibility and was looking for a private party, like the organizing committee, to take the lead. It looked for a time that LA, like Denver would bow out. Finally, the USOC offered to be the partner and share the responsibility.

During the uncertainty, New York City was again considering cautiously whether to jump into the void if need be, though Mayor Ed Koch did not want the city of New York on the hook either. Donald Grant, chairman of the board of the New York Mets, whose Shea Stadium would be part of the venues, objected saying, "The Olympics don't belong in New York and New York can't afford the Olympics." He said using Shea Stadium would violate the Mets lease and they would consider moving. Finally, the USOC offered to be the partner to share the financial responsibility and in February 1979, the games were officially awarded to Los Angeles.

Chapter Seven

Under New Management

"Almost as impressive as the performances by these athletes was that of Lake Placid's hometown organizers...One ominous sign though was the eleven mile traffic jam of spectators going to the competition."

—*Sports Illustrated*, April 1979

B y late December 1978, the ski jumps were ready for competition. Ronald MacKenzie went to the top of the jumps for the opening. After surveying the landscape, he suffered a fatal heart attack. The President of the LPOOC, one of the key men behind the long quest for the games, someone who was a friend and neighbor who had given heart and soul to the community, was gone.

At an emotional funeral for MacKenzie, Rev. Fell eulogized him, explaining why he was one of the leaders pushing for the small town to have the Olympics. "It is in people who dream dreams, people who hope hopes and people who reach for an elusive star." When the LPOOC convened again, Rev. Fell was selected to replace MacKenzie as its President. He and Petr Spurney would have to guide Lake Placid's games in their final year of preparations. Rev. Fell said that he would be able to oversee the business of the committee and that Spurney would focus on the administration of the games.

In Albany, Governor Hugh Carey was sworn into a second term in January after a tough re-election campaign. His Lt. Governor, Mary Ann Krupsak, had challenged him in a Democratic primary. Governor Carey replaced her with Secretary of State Mario Cuomo. The Governor then shuffled his Cabinet, naming Robert Flacke to succeed Peter Berle to head the Department of Environmental Conservation. Environmental groups had written letters to support Berle but he had not been in favor with Carey.

In February, 1979, one year before the games were to begin, there were more pre-Olympic competitions at the new venues with World Cup skiing, and cross country skiing in weather so cold that the daytime temperature hovered around 0 degrees after going as low as 38 below zero one night. Fifty persons were treated for frostbite. Three hundred athletes from 20 countries and 6000 visitors came through the village in a small dress rehearsal for the Olympics. Despite the weather that caused delays in starting competitions, the weekend was a success. Traffic jams with the large number of spectators gave an early indication of problems that would need to be addressed before the games.

Planners knew they would need a well-organized plan for transportation to move spectators as well as workers. Given the limited nature of the roads in and out of the village, it was decided that no spectators' cars would be allowed into the village during the Olympics and that shuttle bus transportation would be arranged for spectators. The LPOOC made plans for transportation expecting that most of the spectators would come as part of bus tour packages operated by travel agencies. To minimize the number of spectators, several events were included in each individual tour package.

Ski jumper at of the Intervale ski jump (author photo)

Spurney said that the LPOOC would have to "build a city bus system" from scratch. Though some accused him of trying to save money on the system, Spurney said that money had not been an issue. He went to Washington to meet with the heads of the major bus lines and asked for a commitment of buses. They were unwilling to do so in light of the energy crisis and the increased demand for passenger service.

Eric Heiden blazed away in Germany and won the 1979 World Speedskating championship for the third consecutive year. In Lake Placid, foreign athletes and officials of their Olympic committees toured the Olympic facilities, including the athletes' village, during the pre-Olympic world competitions. Some of the athletes and their national committees were so shocked by the small quarters that they immediately made arrangements to rent houses during the games rather than stay in the village. An official of the Austrian Olympic team even said that the small, cramped quarters violated the guidelines of the IOC. The Swedes rented four houses and the Italian team rented two houses. The East and West Germans also rented and Norway rented two villas for $30,000. Milan's daily newspaper ran a story headlined, "The Athletes Escape from the the Lake Placid Prison even before entering it."

Ed Stransenback of the LPOOC staff noted it was normal at many Olympics to obtain some outside housing for athletes to relax, particularly the skating federations. However, the dissatisfaction led Mme. Berlioux to decide that national federations, which normally had to pay for athletes' quarters regardless of whether they used them, would not have to do so in Lake Placid. She told *Sports Illustrated*, "This time the accommodations are so poor that delegations will not have to pay for them if they move somewhere else." The LPOOC decided that it would provide more room for the athletes by reducing the number of people in each room and adding several trailers on the grounds with up to six people in each.

In April 1979, the construction controversies took a new twist. Two engineers working for the Economic Development Administration (EDA), Donald Evans and Michael Oliver, became whistleblowers when they went public and said the athletes' village did not meet fire safety codes. At a press conference they said that spectators could be endangered by faultily poured concrete and improper welding at the new arena by the Gilbane Construction Company. Gilbane had been a focus of public scrutiny and ridicule as the general contractor for the Hartford Civic Center which had collapsed in 1978 under the weight of heavy snow. The company said though, that it had not been responsible for the roof.

The whistleblowers said they called the press conference as a last resort because their efforts to have action taken in the Department of Commerce had been unsuccessful. They also said that some members of the LPOOC and the Gilbane Company were resisting the investigation. In May, Evans was then transferred from his job. Gilbane project manager, Ramon Lopez, denied the allegations and said that there had been constant inspections and nothing faulty had been found. The EDA hired an outside engineering firm, Skilling, Hells, Christiansen, and Robertson to conduct an analysis and their report approved the work.

The Lake Placid arena project had been beset by problems and delays including the bankruptcy of McKinney Steel of Albany. McKinney was a family-owned steel fabricator that was "a small company with a big appetite for projects" but was over-committed, said Albany attorney John Starrs who negotiated with its bank to keep it going. Starrs noted the Lake Placid job was an unusual one with tubular construction, which required a high level of perfection in welding. He said that experts were brought in from Alaska because only the construction of the Alaska pipeline and some submarine work provided the kind of experience needed for the job.

Despite all the controversies, the games were fast approaching and all the unresolved issues had to be dealt with. The clock was racing and, by June, the LPOOC had to be ready in just six months to open the games. Final funding of an additional $11 million was approved by Congress and signed off by President Carter. Tickets finally went on sale in July. Allocations of tickets were determined for various regions and groups. The Lake Placid area would get 50,000. The rest of the United States would get 300,000. Canada would get 39,000. All of the other nations would get 39,000. The IOC would have access to 48,000. 74,000 would go to corporate sponsors.

Faced with the need to raise private money, the LPOOC as well as the USOC had embarked on a plan to greatly expand corporate support. This effort was the beginning of the major corporate role in supporting the Olympic Games, which has mushroomed in the years since. Petr Spurney was able to lure some of the big money. He noted, "The tremendous prestige associated with the Olympics provides a marketing advantage to firms who can say they supplied the Olympics." About $25 million was garnered from corporate sponsors through a three-tiered contribution solicitation.

For $50,000, sponsors could use the Olympic rings on their products. For an additional $50,000 products could be promoted with distributors, and for $300,000 sponsors could add promotions and sweepstakes tied to the Olympics. Coca Cola, Nikon, Toshiba, Kodak, and other companies had exclusive rights to have their products called the "official" soft drink or camera for the games. Other companies donated products to be used by athletes and those working at the games.

For many critics, this selling of the Olympics seemed to take away from the idea of promoting Olympic ideals and amateur athletics, but as costs were growing and, without the kind of government support in Communist countries, this appeal for corporate help became attractive for the sponsors as well as the Olympic committees.

By 1984, Peter Ueberroth, the head of the Los Angeles Olympic effort, was able to appeal to corporate sponsors and produce a $224 million profit for the games that the city originally feared would send them into debt like Montreal. Corporate sponsorship is now recognized as a key factor in helping the United States athletes to have the resources for training that has led to better performances in the games with American athletes getting the most medals in the Winter games in Vancouver in 2010.

In August 1979, the USOC announced the great news for Lake Placid that it would be one the USOC official training sites. The announcement ensured that Lake Placid would have an ongoing Olympic role in the future. As the summer came to an end, the major work on the venues including the arena had been completed. On the weekend of September 8th and 9th, the public had its first view of the new 8,500 seat ice arena when an open house was held at all the new venues. The arena project cost $16.2 million, which included the renovation of the 1932 arena.

The US Olympic hockey team had been training at the arena and 1500 watched an intra-squad match and over 3000 watched a figure skating show. Later that month, the arena would host the Flaming Leaves Skate, an international competition and several other events were booked before the Olympics. An unexpected benefit to having the test run in the arena was the discovery of a high level of carbon monoxide in the building. The culprits were the zamboni machines used to clear and smooth the ice. The simple remedy was to start the zambonis outside the building, which was more efficient.

Chapter Eight

On the Eve

"A fever had come over the town"

—*Lake Placid News*, February 1980

T he excitement built in Lake Placid in the fall but there was also nervousness in the air about whether the games would be successful. In mid-November the *New York Times* assessed the mood, "With fewer than 90 days until the Winter Olympics open here, residents are still arguing about whether their village is marching toward a long awaited triumph - or dancing toward disaster." There were predictions that the town could not handle the crowds and there would be massive traffic jams.

Petr Spurney told the *Times*, "I know that many people around here are anxious, fearful, skeptical and that's discouraging. But I can really say that everything is coming together now."

The US hockey team had held tryouts over the summer and had been practicing since the early fall. Then, the team began playing an extensive exhibition hockey schedule against pro and college teams. The team of US collegians, which had never played together until September, was still trying to gel as a unit. Almost all had never participated in international competition. Many were from US Coach Herb Brooks' team at the University of Minnesota. Four were from Boston University including the team captain, Mike Eruzione, star goalie, Jim Craig, Dave Silk and Jack O'Callaghan. Brooks had won three NCAA hockey championships at Minnesota including in 1979. In 1976, Eruzione was on the BU team that lost in the national semifinal game to Brooks' Minnesota team in a game that featured a bench-clearing brawl. BU would win the national championship in 1978.

The Olympic team had an impressive 42-15-3 record in the fall and early winter. Brooks was a tough disciplinarian who was earning the outright wrath of his players because he pushed them so hard, but they were getting better and began to believe that they might just be a surprise. A tournament was held at the new Olympic arena just before Christmas. The US team came from behind and beat both Sweden and Canada in front of an arena that was half full but enthusiastic in supporting the US team.

Then, they had to play Czechoslovakia and the Soviet Union, the top two teams in the world. The US team shut out the Czechs and came from behind to shock the Soviets, 5-3, before a wildly cheering home crowd. The US team swept the tournament on the ice where the Olympics would be held two months later. Much credit was given to the superb play of goalie Jim Craig and the US team had high hopes of achieving its goal of getting a medal in February.

Just like in 1932, there was very little snow in the early winter as the calendar turned to January 1980 and a new decade began. In the weeks leading up to the opening of the games, tour operators reported that they had hundreds of tickets still available. The *Toronto Globe and Mail* ran a story saying the skiing events might be moved to Quebec if there was no snow in Lake Placid. However, the LPOOC had no such plans since it always claimed the artificial snow-making equipment they had acquired "weather-proofed" the games. Finally, six inches of snow came on January 28.

The issue of the new arena's structural integrity arose again in January as David Evans, the engineer with the US Commerce Department, charged in an unauthorized news conference that there were still safety concerns. Gilbane Construction reviewed Evans' concerns and decided to put up two additional steel trusses between the first and second levels of the arena. The facility had been judged safe by the Skilling firm in August but the company's engineer later said he had seen inaccurate architectural drawings and said the facility could be unsafe.

Many local residents were tired of all the controversies and disruptions in their daily lives. By the time the games were ready to begin, some in the town couldn't wait until they were over and life in the village could return to a more normal existence. "There were many who weren't happy with the way things went in January. Too much politicking, too much confusion, and too much intrusion. If the Olympics were put up for a vote last month, I believe the townspeople would have voted them down," said Police Chief Horace Pratt on the eve of the games.

Excitement built though as the game approached and athletes from other countries began to arrive. The Olympic athletes' village of eleven buildings behind twelve foot high monitored fences opened on January 28. Despite all the controversy about it becoming a prison, it became a place where young athletes shared each other's company. They spent their free time playing electronic games and relaxing. It had a discotheque, a 300 seat movie theater, some live entertainment, games rooms, dining rooms, a sauna, exercise room and gift shop. Most of the athletes found it small but adequate and enjoyed mingling with their peers from around the world. The Chinese athletes enjoyed watching old western movies. Two hundred and fifty New York State Police troopers were assigned to patrol the athletes' village and a group of "biosensor" German shepherds checked for explosives.

Though the Lake Placid games would not begin until February 12, the prelude to the games began in Greece on January 28. Rev. Fell, Congressman McEwen, Chris Ortloff and other members and staff of the LPOOC went to Olympia, Greece where the Olympic torch was lit for its journey to the United States and Lake Placid. A 1000 mile torch relay would take place by runners carrying the Olympic flame from the Langley Air Force Base in Virginia where it arrived from Greece aboard Air Force One. This was the first time in four Olympic Games held in the United States that the Olympic torch for the games had been lit in Greece. There had been no torch relay for the 1932 games.

Six thousand people applied to be runners to carry the Olympic torch. Fifty-two runners were chosen for four teams running three to five miles each. Three ran together, one with the flame, one with an American flag and one with the Olympic flag. The relay took nine days, passing through the nation's capital and up the Middle Atlantic States with stops in Baltimore, Wilmington, Delaware, the Philadelphia Art Museum, Princeton University and then was met by hundreds of schoolchildren at City Hall Park in New York after a Lake Placid veterinarian, Robert Lopez, carried it across the Brooklyn Bridge.

Then, it went up the Hudson River with a stop at the FDR home and library in Hyde Park and on to Albany for a ceremony that was held at the State Capitol on February 6 in the middle of the day. Ten thousand state workers and local residents joined Governor Carey as the torch was lit in a makeshift cauldron at the Empire State Plaza. It would stay lit in Albany for the duration of the days before and during the games.

Albany crowd at the Empire State Plaza after Olympic torch lit en route to Lake Placid (author photo)

Two torches were lit in Albany and from there, the runners continued and split in Warrensburg as they entered the Adirondack Park. They would take two routes through the Adirondacks to Lake Placid so that more of the residents of the Adirondacks could observe the torch as it made its final approach to the Olympic village.

All 52 runners were present on Friday night, February 8th as the torch arrived in Lake Placid. Thousands of people jammed Main Street as the two final runners made their way into town. Eight thousand people attended the Torch Arrival Ceremony at the speed skating oval in front of Lake Placid High School, adjacent to the new arena, where Jack Shea lit the cauldron.

Now, it felt like the Olympics had arrived and the *Lake Placid News* editorialized that "a "fever had come over the town."

Chapter Nine

International Politics

"I did not want to damage the Olympic movement, but at the same time it seemed unconscionable to be guests of the Soviets while they were involved in a bloody suppression of the people of Afghanistan - an act condemned by an overwhelming majority of the nations of the world. It was not an easy decision."

—President Jimmy Carter in his book *Keeping Faith*

I n November 1979, America was thrown into crisis when Iranian students seized the American embassy in Tehran and took over forty American diplomats and employees hostage. Then, at the end of December 1979, less than two months before the games in Lake Placid were scheduled to begin, and seven years after the tragedy in Munich, international events again intruded on the Olympics. The Soviet Union invaded Afghanistan in a stunning move that seemed to take advantage of the United States-Iranian hostage crisis that started in November. The Soviets, fearing the growing influence of Islamic fundamentalist rebels, were siding with a socialist regime it had been supporting and wanted to prop up for fear it could lose control of the country.

History has since defined the Cold War as ending with the fall of the Berlin Wall and the resulting fall of Communism in eastern Europe and the Soviet Union itself. By the winter of 1980, the Cold War had receded and citizens of the United States and the Soviet Union no longer lived on edge like during the early 1960s when the Berlin Wall was built and the Cuban Missile Crisis had the nation on the verge of a possible nuclear war.

In the 1970s, President Richard Nixon had launched a policy of "detente" with the Soviets and the Chinese in the early 1970s. Still, the Soviets were ruled in 1980 by Leonid Brezhnev and an older generation who grew up during the early days of the Communist revolution. They had lived through World War II and the early days of the Cold War and the Stalin era. International tensions could quickly erupt in global hot spots of tension and the atmosphere of the Cold War would return.

Such was the case at the end of 1979 and early 1980. Every night the evening news reported how many days the US hostages had been in captivity in Iran. President Carter cancelled all of his travel engagements and stayed in Washington throughout the crisis, even refusing to join the campaign trail in Democratic primaries in a tough fight for re-election against Senator Edward Kennedy who challenged him for the party's nomination. President Carter had indicated his intention in 1978 to attend the Olympics but that plan was likely to be changed.

Moscow Olympic mascot

Carter immediately demanded that the Soviets pull their troops out of Afghanistan and on January

4, 1980, for the first time, he publicly tied the invasion to the Summer Olympics, which were slated to be held later in 1980 in Moscow. Carter had agreed to a controversial grain embargo against the Soviets. However, the President viewed a boycott of the Summer Olympics as the ultimate sanction and leverage because of the national pride that the Soviets had derived from being chosen to host the Summer Olympic Games for the first time. Soon, Carter urged the International Olympic Committee to re-schedule the games somewhere else and suggested two other possible sites, Montreal and Melbourne, Australia.

The United States even suggested that the Olympics should have a permanent home, perhaps in Greece to avoid international problems and also to save money by not having to build new facilities, which were becoming too expensive for most cities. Within days, the Greek government stated that it would support such a move to eventually locate the games in their nation, where the Olympics began, to save them from "political and commercial exploitation."

Carter wrote in *Keeping Faith*, his autobiography of his time in office,

Before making a decision, I held many meetings with my advisers and consulted closely with other heads of state and with sports leaders in our country....I announced our decision about the Moscow Olympics on a "Meet the Press" interview show on January 20. We would send a message with copies to other government leaders in the world, stating that unless the Soviets withdraw their troops from Afghanistan within a month, there should be no participation in the Moscow games...I knew the decision was controversial but I had no idea at the time how difficult it would be for me to implement it or convince other nations to join us.

The Olympic movement, despite its idealism and desire to be free of politics, had been tormented for decades by international tensions. The games were canceled during World War I. Iron-ically, there was intense fighting going on as the Third Winter Olympics were underway in Lake Placid in 1932. Japan had invaded China but there was no call then to ban Japan from the games. In 1936, a year after Germany had adopted its anti-Semitic Nuremburg laws, Jews and human rights advocates urged that the summer games be moved from Berlin where Hitler served as host. World War II broke out a few years after the Berlin games and the Olympics were cancelled in 1940 and 1944. Germany and nations that were defeated in both world wars were not invited to participate in the years after those wars.

In 1956, the Netherlands, Spain and Switzerland boycotted the summer games in Melbourne to protest the Soviet invasion of Hungary. In 1976, twenty countries stayed away from Montreal to protest the presence of New Zealand. New Zealand had played rugby tournaments with South Africa, which was ostra-cized internationally for its apartheid race policies. South Africa was banned from competition from 1964 until 1992 when Nelson Mandela brought change to the country. Ironically, when the winter games returned to the United States in Salt Lake City in 2002, American troops were fighting in Afghanistan, invading the country after the September 11, 2001 terrorist attacks. The Republic of Georgia called for a boycott of the 2014 winter games in Sochi because of the South Ossetia War with Russia in 2008.

There were just weeks between the Soviet invasion and the open-ing of the Lake Placid games where the International Olympic Committee would be meeting to discuss Carter's request. The USOC felt tremendous pressure from Carter's advocacy of a boy-cott. At first, it resisted and said that there was no way that an alternate games could be arranged. The USOC was in a terrible spot, caught between its allegiance to the Olympic movement and the United States. The IOC rules were clear that national Olympic committees were not to be instruments of their govern-ments or to bow to national political pressures. Of course, those guidelines had long been ignored in Communist countries and countries with authoritarian governments.

The USOC committee sent a telegram to the President saying they opposed the boycott. Robert Kane, President of the USOC, said the boycott could destroy the Olympic movement. The USOC met with Secretary of State Cyrus Vance and, after it was clear that the President was going forward with his call of a boycott, the USOC became reluctantly supportive.

President Carter sent a letter to Robert Kane, "I would support the participation of athletes from the entire world at Summer Olympics or other games this summer outside the Soviet Union, just as I welcome athletes from the entire world to Lake Placid, for the winter games." He called for all nations to support a permanent home in Greece for the summer games and to find an appropriate site for the winter games.

"This is the last Olympics. It is all President Carter's fault," a Swedish fan complained to Lise Bang Jensen, a reporter for the *Knickerbocker News* in Albany. Jack Shea, Lake Placid's 1932 skating hero was disappointed with the infringement of international politics into the Olympics and disappointed with President Carter's position, "The Olympics is an ecumenical family of international getting together for friendly competition. To use the Olympics games as a toll to achieve a political purpose is unfortunate."

Senator Edward Kennedy, who was in the midst of his Presidential campaign challenge against Carter, did not support the boycott and felt US athletes should go to Moscow and beat the Soviets. Republican candidate Ronald Reagan, who would be elected President in part because of the Iran hostage crisis and famously had called the Soviet Union the "evil empire," supported the boycott at first but then backed off saying it was unfair to the athletes.

The executive board of the USOC rapidly moved to support Carter's request and voted unanimously on January 26 to ask the IOC to postpone, cancel or move the Moscow games. A group of 50 Olympic athletes wanted the United States to pursue a total economic boycott of the Soviet Union as a more effective measure than the Olympic boycott. They felt like political pawns caught in a terrible dilemma whatever happened. Staying home meant giving up their Olympic dreams, but going to Moscow would be viewed as unpatriotic and would actually be seen as a slap in the face to the US government. It would also be seen as tacitly supportive of Moscow's attempt to be accepted by the world community while also having invaded a foreign country.

On February 8 USOC President Robert Kane said that contract between the IOC and the Moscow organizing committee had been broken and it was impossible for Moscow to "fulfill the aims of the Olympic movement." The Olympic games should not be held in the capital of a country at war," Kane said, echoing Carter's view.

There was concern among members of the USOC that if the United States boycotted Moscow that the Soviets would likely boycott the summer games in Los Angeles in 1984. And, if the US moved ahead too quickly and announced a boycott before the winter games, the Soviet Union might boycott the Lake Placid games too. Instead of announcing an immediate boycott, an ultimatum was delivered to the Soviets to withdraw their troops by February 20 or the United States would boycott the Moscow games.

Petr Spurney was never concerned that the Soviets might not show up. He knew how much the Soviets valued their role in the IOC and the place of their officials and judges. If the Soviets boycotted the games, they would lose their status in all those roles.

There were other concerns that the Soviets would be banned from entering the country for the Lake Placid games. President

Carter did not intend to block them from participating at Lake Placid and the Soviet team did not want politics interfering with their Olympic team. It would have been foolish for the Soviets to boycott Lake Placid anyway because they would have assured a US boycott of the Moscow games. Those games were still months away and possibilities still existed for something to change.

Lord Killanin, upon arriving in Lake Placid from his home in Dublin for the Winter Games in February and the meeting of the International Olympic Committee, called it "one of the most critical sessions of the IOC since its foundation in 1894." He also said that the word "boycott" was the bane of his existence. Killanin said that he still felt that moving the Moscow games was "legally and technically impossible."

The Lake Placid games, which once seemed so improbable, were now ready to begin. But as the *Washington Post* reported on February 2, 1980, Lake Placid "also finds itself playing host to Games that the more apocalyptic commentators are calling 'the last Olympics' because the US boycott of the Moscow games would destroy the Olympics as they have been known." Art Devlin agreed, saying "Lake Placid could be the last Olympics in our lifetime."

As the games opened, the *New York Times* editorialized in support of moving the summer games to Greece and neutral Switzerland in the winter to end the nationalism, commercialism and threats of terrorism. It said the IOC cannot avoid politics,

"The lopsided vote in Congress urging a boycott of the Moscow Games is a reminder that the world can never really go away. If such signals are ignored, the IOC may not have to worry about politics much longer. For the Olympics could become, more easily than some fans appear to realize, a matter of memory, and Lake Placid the last of the wine."

Though the Soviet's Afghanistan invasion and proposed boycott was the focus of concern regarding the Summer Olympics in

Moscow, another international issue tormented the IOC regarding the Winter Olympics as the Lake Placid games drew near: what to do about China. The Peoples' Republic of China had avoided the Olympic Games in the past but now wanted to participate. They were approved to appear in the winter games for the first time since 1948 before the Communist government of Mao took over. Taiwan, or Nationalist China, also wanted to participate and believed it should be the true representative of China. In 1976, Canadian authorities refused to give the Taiwanese visas to enter the country for the Montreal Olympics because of pressure from the Communist government in Peking, as it was known then.

The IOC had worked for months on trying to resolve the issue at Lake Placid and thought it had a solution when it asked Taiwan to attend with a different anthem and flag under the name Chinese Taipei. When they refused, the IOC barred them from participating in the games. The Taiwanese went to a court in Plattsburgh, New York, which held that the IOC decision was discriminatory and ruled Taiwan could take part with its own flag, anthem and name. That decision was reversed by another court just before the games opened and Taiwan refused to attend. Some wondered why two Chinas could not participate in the games since there were two Germanys who participated. Taiwan finally relented in 1984 and took part as Chinese Taipei.

As the games drew near, one group of Soviet athletes arrived on Tuesday night, February 5, on buses from Montreal following a flight from Moscow. Sergei Pavlov, President of the Soviet Olympic Committee told the *New York Times*, when asked if the boycott would destroy the Olympic movement, "I think everybody who loves sports and the ideals of the Olympic movement thinks it will." Another group of 122 Soviet athletes flew into JFK airport on Sunday night and had to be sent to Dulles International Airport in Washington after baggage handlers for Pan Am refused to service the Soviet Aeroflot plane to protest the Soviet invasion of Afghanistan. Five star athletes wrote a letter to the Soviet newspaper *Izvestia* to protest their treatment, an obvious effort by the Soviets to bring attention to the incident.

It was noticeable to reporters that the Soviet athletes and entourage in Lake Placid were an uptight bunch. They kept to themselves and did not partake of much publicly outside of their athletic contests. Perhaps it was because there were being watched. Whenever athletes went outside the country, there were certainly KGB and security personnel with them and they did not want to be observed doing anything that would be reported to their superiors.

Petr Spurney remembered how a "safe house" had been established secretly in Lake Placid, which would be ready for any athletes from the Soviet Union or elsewhere who wanted to defect during the games. Spurney said there were rumors that one Soviet skater might be interested.

When they arrived in Lake Placid, the Soviet athletes knew nothing of President Carter's boycott threat of the summer games. A woman athlete from the Soviet Union told the *Lake Placid News* that she had seen some of the boycott signs but said "they were the work of hooligans." Though most athletes preferred to talk about sports and not politics, she asked if the American press had reported that the Afghan government, which had a treaty with the Soviet Union, had invited the Soviets into their country to help defend it as the treaty required and she alluded to the United States doing the same thing to help Vietnam not so many years earlier.

That sentiment was also voiced by IOC Director Monique Berlioux who said that the United States was fighting in Vietnam in 1970 when the IOC awarded the 1976 winter games to Denver. When Lake Placid won the games in 1974, it was still in Cambodia, she noted.

The LPOOC was also concerned about the security of the Soviet athletes and wanted to take precautions against any hostile acts or unpleasant incidents by spectators. Just two days before the games, bomb smelling security dogs were deployed in the new Olympic arena before the Soviet team was to practice. When the Russians played Japan in hockey on the opening night, the American audience yelled, "Go home Ruskies, go home." A man raised enough money to buy full page ads of the Afghanistan flag to be in the *Lake Placid News* throughout the games. He wanted spectators to wave the flags at the Soviet athletes.

With memories of Munich still fresh from 1972, overall security remained a big concern. In 1932, there were four horses and 53 state troopers at the 1932 games. As the games opened in 1980, there were 1000 state and federal police, razor ribbon fences, and television security monitors in addition to the dogs. US Attorney General Benjamin Civiletti arrived in Lake Placid the week before the games to review the security plans.

Secret Service agents and staff from the Immigration and Naturalization Service (INS) were on duty and had been through joint training exercises in early December against several types of terrorist attacks. The State Police had been trained on skis in case of a terrorist attack in the mountains. US military forces were also available if needed if an attack occurred. They also helped with support services. Dogs were deployed when supply trucks entered the athletes' village and there were three metal detectors in the village that everyone had to pass through.

Despite all the security, the biggest threat did not seem to be terrorists though. Instead it was local youths who enjoyed arson. In the weeks before the games, there were five fires reported at the Lake Placid Resort Hotel where the IOC would be staying.

On Sunday night, February 10, just two days before the games were to begin, the IOC met at that same hotel. *New York Times* columnist Dave Anderson noted how out of touch with international events and political realities the IOC seemed to be. "Of its 89 members the committee has four princes, four generals, two lords, a sheik, a rajah, a knight, a count, a baron, a marquis, a duke an admiral and a hadju. There are no women."

After Lord Killanin opened the meeting by saying, "We sincerely hope these Games will not be used for the furtherance of political aims, or demonstrations of prejudices," he called on US Secretary of State Cyrus Vance to speak. Vance noted that there was a "truce of the Gods " in the ancient Olympics and that "during this truce open warfare against or by the host city was forbidden."

He then made his main point and the reason for his presence, the President's concern about Afghanistan. Vance was direct and blunt, "Let me make my Government's position clear. We will oppose the participation of an American team in any Olympic games in the capital of an invading nation. This position is firm. It reflects the deep convictions of the United States Congress and the American people. To avoid such problems in the future, we support the establishment of a permanent home for the Summer and Winter Olympics." Vance suggested alternate games be developed.

Anderson concluded in his article, "A boycott will embarrass the International Olympic Committee whose members are not accustomed to existing in the real world." Some of the IOC members were appalled by Vance's bluntness and thought he was rude. In their minds, he was supposed to be there in a ceremonial role representing the President of the host country and to give welcoming remarks. Sharing the same sense as Anderson, Vance would later remark, "The IOC committee itself is really quite divorced from the real world. It's its own little group that picks its own successors. I think it really has pretty much lost touch with reality and really doesn't realize the political consequences of the issues involved."

There were some who were eager for reform including a 30-year member of the IOC, Count de Beaumont of France. He wanted the IOC to take up his suggestions for drastic reform of the games, eliminating the nationalism by having athletes compete as individuals and with clubs as was done in the earliest Olympics. He wanted the president of the IOC to open the games, not the leader of the host country. He wanted the athletes to walk into the opening ceremonies without national flags, which could be placed together in the center of the arena.

Julian Roosevelt, a US member of the IOC who had participated in the yachting events at the 1952 summer games, accused President Carter of engaging in election year politics in his effort to boycott the summer games. "The world 'Olympics, until Mr. Carter got hold of it, was good." Now, its synonymous with Communist. Roosevelt also criticized the IOC for failing to permit Taiwan to participate.

Petr Spurney attended the IOC session and said that Vance's remarks "created a pall with the IOC and changed the tenor politically of events." He was "totally disappointed by the cloud" over the games but would have to make the "best of a terrible situation." After Vance's presentation, the IOC met and decided it could not and would not do anything to cancel or move the games from Moscow. Carter's ultimatum that the Soviets had to withdraw from Afghanistan by February 20, still stood. The United States could announce such a boycott right in the middle of the Lake Placid games.

While the IOC was preparing to meet in Lake Placid, a final exhibition game against the Soviet Union was set for Saturday, February 9th at Madison Square Garden. There had been a lot of discussion about cancelling it because of security concerns. All packages brought into the building were searched. US Coach Herb Brooks was concerned about security and whether there would be any incidents at the game.

There were no incidents and the Soviet team trounced the USA team, 10-3, having an easy time breaking the US defense. The Soviets took a 4-0 lead after the first period. Coach Herb Brooks said it was his fault they loss. "I gave them a bad plan." The Soviet Coach, Viktor Tikhonov, said "Today, we showed what we could do but they did not." The Soviets had every reason to be confident they would win a fifth consecutive hockey gold medal in the days ahead.

Eric Heiden spent the weekend before the games competing in the World Sprint Speedskating championships in his hometown, West Allis Wisconsin. Heiden would win the competition with overall points but not before losing one of the races to fellow American, Tom Plant.

Students at Lake Placid High School had already begun a five week vacation for the games. Many schools would close and students would work in supporting roles during the games. There were 6700 volunteers including students who were being deployed to help with the games.

As the games were set to open, a round-trip bus ticket from the Holiday Turf Inn in Albany for the first day of the competition, with two hockey games and lunch, cost $70, tax and gratuity included. A ticket to a hockey playoff game on Friday, February 22 would cost $110. No one knew it would be "the" game between the United States and the Soviet Union.

On Monday, two days before the Opening Ceremonies, travel restrictions began. The new bus transportation system went into operation and, immediately, trouble started. With only 80 of 300 buses operating, there were delays and many workers could not reach their workplaces on time. Some reporters were stranded at Whiteface Mountain and hitchhiked back to Lake Placid. Buses were an hour and a half late though they were supposed to arrive every fifteen minutes. Petr Spurney expressed "absolute faith" that the system would work.

Though the official opening of the games wouldn't take place until the Opening Ceremonies on Wednesday afternoon, February 13, competition was underway the night before with several hockey matches. Less than 1000 fans watched the first competition between Canada and the Netherlands.

Testing of the athletes for drugs and gender identity also was being prepared after each race. A staff of forty chemists and bio-chemists would work to test athletes after each race. Drug test-ing had begun at Grenoble and eleven athletes tested positively with drug infractions at the Montreal games. There were no vio-lations in Lake Placid of the 440 tests taken. Tests for gender identification continued at Lake Placid because, over the years, there were allegations of men trying to compete as women in order to win. In Montreal, only Britain's Princess Anne who was on the equestrian team was exempted from the testing, which was stopped in later years because of ethical and privacy concerns.

Chapter Ten
Let the Games Begin

The singular essence of the Olympic Games is that the world takes the same stage at the same time, performing a passion play of nations, races, ideologies, talents, styles, and aspirations that no other venue, not even the United Nations, can match.

—David Maraniss, Rome 1960

After decades of bidding, years of planning and building and months of controversy and second guessing, Lake Placid was ready to again take its place on the stage of international sports competition - and international politics. Much had changed in the world and in the Olympics since the athletes had gathered in Lake Placid in 1932. The world had become smaller and more mobile.

Having grown up in northern New York and vacationed in the Adirondacks, what a great thrill it was in February 1980 to see the opening of ABC's coverage of the Winter Olympics in Lake Placid. Jim McKay, the legendary anchor, narrated an aerial view up the Hudson River from New York City with the World Trade Center towers in its skyline, through the Catskills, over the State Capitol in Albany, my current home, and on up into the Adirondacks all the way to Lake Placid and Whiteface Mountain . There in the land of snowcapped peaks and timeless beauty the world had come for the Thirteenth Winter Games.

ABC Sports had 800 employees in Lake Placid with 109 cameras to televise 51 ½ hours of both live coverage of events in the evening in the United States along with taped coverage from earlier events each day. All advertising had been sold. ABC had to lay miles of cable to cover the skiing events on Whiteface Mountain, fighting porcupines and other animals that liked to chew it up. 1800 foreign journalists were at the press center to report and send stories to nations around the world.

On Wednesday, February 13, 1980, at 2:00 p.m. the Opening Ceremonies of the Thirteenth Winter Olympic Games began at the temporary stadium built on the flat valley surrounded by high peaks where the Lake Placid Horse Show was held every summer. The field was adjacent to the private Lake Placid airport where private planes take off on scenic tours. Surrounding that flat field were magnificent views of majestic mountains, including Whiteface Mountain. This site was selected by the LPOOC as the best site for the ceremonies after the LPOOC considered the Intervale ski jump area and the skating oval in front of the high school, which was the location for the opening ceremonies in 1932. The morning newspapers and network news reported that it was Day 100 of the Iranian hostage crisis with no end to the standoff. Iran had been issued an invitation to participate at Lake Placid but had never responded.

The LPOOC had conducted a major rehearsal of the Opening Ceremonies three months earlier on November 4, 1979 and then again on January 26. There had been a moderate snowfall the night before and the weather was blustery for the ceremony, not too cold but with a wind to lift and flutter all the national flags. The visibility was clear enough to see the range of mountains including Whiteface. On the air, Jim McKay wondered whether there would be another Olympics with all the international tension and talk of boycott.

Twenty-three thousand people made their way to the site, including Vice President Walter Mondale who arrived by helicopter to represent President Carter. Despite President Carter's commitment in 1978, to attend the Opening Ceremonies, he had made a decision not to travel much in order to demonstrate his complete focus on the hostage crisis in Iran. Three months after the crisis began, he was being criticized for becoming a "hostage" himself as the crisis dragged on and he refused to allow himself to take part in important national events like the Olympics.

Petr Spurney had recruited Tommy Walker, Vice President of Entertainment, for Walt Disney who worked with Chris Ortloff, Chair of the Ceremonies Committee, to add color and action to the ceremonies. The *New York Times* reported that, "the pageantry was traditional, lavish and sometimes spectacular with skydivers trailing plumes of raspberry-colored smoke leaping from planes before the ceremonies began."

There was a 120 piece orchestra, a 450 voice choir, a drum corps and a marching band. Some of the athletes were waiting for more than an hour in the cold for buses to take them to the ceremonies. The procession into the outdoor stadium began, as always, with Greece which held the first Olympics. Then, the countries marched in alphabetical order. There were 1282 athletes from the 37 countries who would compete in 38 events.

Just a few weeks before the games, it was revealed that the Canadian ambassador and embassy staff in Tehran had hidden six American diplomatic staff who had evaded being captured and made it to the Canadian embassy. In its first secret session since World War II, the Canadian Parliament approved special Canadian passports for the Americans. The Americans were able to sneak out and left Tehran on a flight to Zurich, Switzerland on January 28. The American people were extremely grateful for this brave act and the Olympics provided the first public opportunity to pay tribute. A huge ovation greeted the Canadian athletes as they entered the stadium for the Opening Ceremonies.

The American athletes would enter the stadium last, wearing tan, western style jackets with white cowboy style hats. They were led by a little known 21 year-old figure skater, Scott Hamilton, who had a cystic fibrosis type disease since childhood and took up skating for therapy. Skating became a cure and his American teammates wanted Hamilton as their inspirational leader. Some of his friends pulled him out of the movie theater on Main Street in Lake Placid a few days before the games as if something was terribly wrong. Instead they told Hamilton that had been picked for the honor of carrying the flag.

In his autobiography, *Landing It*, Hamilton remembered,

"Even though they took my measurements, every piece of clothing I had on was too big, which made my role even more potentially disastrous. My mittens were so large it was hard to get a grip on the flagpole. My hat was about three sizes too big and it kept slipping down my forehead. My boots were so oversize I had to wear two pairs of wool socks."

He would finish fifth in the men's figure skating competition in Lake Placid, but he would win the gold medal four years later in Sarajevo. As a professional, he led the Stars on Ice tour, which trained every year in Lake Placid and then gave its first tour performance at the Olympic Arena.

Eight past US Olympians carried in the Olympic flag: figure skaters, Dick Button, Dr. Tenley Albright, speed skaters, Jack Shea and Sheila Young, skiers Andrea Mead Lawrence and Barbara Ann Cochran, Willie Davenport and Al Oerter, four-time discus throw winner. Davenport, who had won a decathlon medal in the summer games, was the first African-American winter games athlete for the US. Eric Heiden took the Olympic oath on behalf of all the athletes.

Rev. Fell addressed the ceremonies on behalf of the LPOOC and said,

"We would like to somehow make the beginning of these games signal the beginning of a new understanding among the peoples of all nations. For this to happen, we need help....We would be prouder still, the people of this village and the members of our organizing committee, if we could say that what we did contributed toward the preservation of the Olympics. And, even more importantly, toward the preservation of world peace."

Governor Carey welcomed the athletes, speakers and attendees on behalf of the State of New York. He noted in his remarks that the region had been a place of "healing" referring to the tuberculosis sanitariums in nearby Saranac Lake, and he hoped that legacy would benefit the international community.

Ed Hale of the *Watertown Daily Times* wrote that the Russians and American athletes were happy after the applause as they entered and stood almost side by side, separated only by Yugoslavia. "The bear rubbed shoulders with the eagle."

While that happened, there was a small protest against the Soviet invasion of Afghanistan. STOP activists released hundreds of balloons protesting the planned prison conversion.

As the ceremony ended, 2,000 doves were released along with thousands of helium balloons, which flew into the Adirondack sky, intended as a symbol of peace even though the immediate controversy between the United States and the Soviet Union threatened the summer games. The *Lake Placid News* observed, "Behind the prism of athletes, flags and uniforms, 25,000 bright little balloons floated skyward like a bag of confetti defying gravity."

More signs of looming trouble with transportation were becoming apparent even at the Opening Ceremonies. There were not enough buses to transport all the spectators back to the village and many were stranded. Some had to walk two and a half miles back to downtown Lake Placid. LPOOC counsel Bill Kissel and Watertown attorney Mike Schell recalled the hard wooden bleachers they sat on during the Opening Ceremonies and then walking back to town. Kissel had a permit to drive in the village and had driven over to the Opening Ceremonies but gave up trying to drive back because of the crowds in the street. One State Police official said the exodus after the Opening Ceremonies was worse than what happened at Woodstock eleven years earlier when there were more than ten times as many people.

Meanwhile, 1000 persons were stranded at Whiteface Mountain after watching downhill skiing. Two hundred thirty-seven buses were available but were ordered not to idle in the parking lot. So, the buses continued to drive around, so all were not able to get back in time with the crowds.

The Adirondack Railway from Utica was two hours late and its passengers arrived in time only to see the second half of the Opening Ceremonies. They traveled twelve and half hours to see thirty minutes but many of them were train buffs who enjoyed riding the restored line.

The days before the Olympics began, there were signs around town saying, "Welcome World, We're Ready." Within a few days those signs were ridiculed and the euphoria of the games was overwhelmed by a breakdown in the transportation system. In the first few days of the competition, buses did not move people on time and many missed the events they had tickets for. The LPOOC had to exchange or refund tickets. Hundreds stood outside in the cold waiting for buses that never came. Some of the bus drivers who were from downstate and other areas got lost because they were unfamiliar with the Lake Placid region.

The bus situation was compounded by the traffic on the roads that slowed the buses. While no cars were generally allowed in a radius outside of Lake Placid, local traffic was allowed for the local residents. Some had friends and guests from out of town who came into town prior to the games. Others had rented their homes to people who drove into town to stay. State Police were checking to make sure only those with permits were driving in the area.

In those days before cellphones, the landline telephone system, which was handling more calls than the middle of Manhattan at the same time, broke down. The system was supposed to be able to handle 11,000 calls per hour in and out of Lake Placid, and when over 12,000 were made as the games began, New York Telephone Company scrambled to quickly add more lines.

The transportation problems were compounded by another mistake. While international politics may not have ruffled IOC feathers, botching an awards ceremony did. Each night, the medals were to be given out on a stage at a ten foot high "crystal pavilion" on the ice of Mirror Lake near the town beach. On the second night, Soviet medal winning athletes missed the awards ceremony because they were not informed about it. Spurney apologized to Killanin and said it was an error. Also the flags could not be raised for the countries of the winning athletes because they did not fit in to the moorings on the ice.

The awards ceremonies were properly carried off for the rest of the games and became a highlight of the day with fireworks after the awards program with as many as 10,000 attending on some nights.

While the transportation problems continued into the first full day of competition, Eric Heiden methodically went about his preparations and then proceeded to break the Olympic record and win the gold medal in the 500 meter race. On Saturday, Heiden won the 5000 meter race. Many speed skaters do not compete in all the races like Heiden had intended to. So, many of the other 5000 meter racers were rested, having not skated in the 500 meter race. Heiden's sister, Beth, had also dreamed of winning a gold medal but had to settle for a third place finish and a bronze medal. Leah Poulos-Mueller would win two silver medals in speed skating for the United States.

Americans were disappointed when pairs figure skater Randy Gardner suffered an injury.. He warmed up on the arena ice and fell in all his attempts to jump. The crowd was stunned when it was announced that he and his partner, Tai Babalonia, had withdrawn from the competition that they had been preparing for several years. There had been great anticipation of their battle against the Soviet pairs team of Irina Rodina and Alexander Zaitsev, who went on to win the gold medal, the fifth straight Soviet couple to do so in pairs. Americans were also hoping for a gold medal from ladies skater Linda Fratiane.

Meanwhile the United States hockey team, which had ranked seventh of the twelve teams before the games, kept winning after its opening game with Sweden that was held the night before the opening ceremonies. The US team was trailing Sweden, 2-1, late in that game when Dave Silk scored with 27 seconds left and gave the team a tie. The arena was not full that night but those attending enthusiastically began a cheer heard for the first time in Olympic competition, "USA, USA, USA."

The hockey competition had been set up with two divisions of six teams. The top two teams in each division would go to the medal round on the closing weekend. Not only was it important to win, but also to score as many goals as possible since that would be one criteria for a tiebreaker if necessary to determine which of two teams with the same record would advance. So, the Soviet team took advantage of the rules and opened with a 18-0 trouncing of Japan. The US hockey team proved it was no lightweight with a stunning victory over powerhouse Czechoslovakia, 7-3. People began to take notice because the Czech team was considered the second best after the Soviets. In fact, those two teams plus Sweden were considered the top three teams in the tournament.

The transportation problem was an inconvenient disaster for spectators but it was a public relations disaster for the Olympics and the LPOOC. It was not surprising that in the first few days of the games, the bus situation dominated international reporting about the games and relegated the results of some of the contests to inside pages of local papers. "We have failed you, there is no question," said Ed Lewi, spokesman for the games. Rev. Fell said that the LPOOC had tried to save too much on the buses. Petr Spurney explained, "Spectators should expect some inconvenience. Winter sports are rugged events." He says now that the failure of the bus system "still upsets me."

Newspapers were providing extensive coverage of the games but some columnists blasted ABC's coverage and anchor Jim McKay for not reporting the depth of the problems in their broadcasts, sticking to the feel good stories about the athletes and the Olympics. ABC was broadcasting across the country and responded that, while the bus story might have been newsworthy, the viewers were not affected and were more interested in the competition and the aura of the Olympics themselves.

People began to wonder if Lake Placid had truly bitten off more than it could chew. "Had the weather been close to what it was in 1979, the casualties at that parking lot and in other freezing areas might been close to those in Afghanistan," observed E.J Kahn, Jr. in the *New Yorker* magazine.

Rev. Fell, at an emergency meeting of the LPOOC on Thursday night, February 14, to consider closing the games to all spectators because of his fear that the situation was dangerous and could be life threatening for those stranded in the cold. Such a decision, though, would have certainly resulted in the LPOOC being viewed as an incompetent failure and perhaps the games in Lake Placid viewed as a mistaken decision. His proposal was not adopted and Ed Lewi told the press that Rev. Fell didn't really mean it.

Ed Lewi was bearing the brunt of the media questions. He admitted that the transportation crisis was the fault of the committee and that the person in charge "just didn't do the job." Greyhound said it had offered just two weeks before the games to provide technical assistance to the LPOOC to help.

By the weekend, the transportation situation continued to decline as interest in the games increased. The round-the-clock media coverage led many persons trying to drive into the area to take the buses and buy tickets. This was not the case in the first few days when tickets were still available and many of the events were not filled to their capacity.

The LPOOC had misjudged how people would get to the games. They expected half of those attending would come on charter buses that would move right into the village and would not need the bus transportation arranged. However, it turned out that most people came by car and parked in the peripheral lots and intended to use the buses to get into the venues. Some did not even have tickets and were not supposed to be allowed on the buses. However, they got through and added to the overload. Some tour operators sold extra tickets separately outside of their tour bus packages and those ticket holders would need to ride the public buses. By Sunday, thousands had to wait more than an hour for buses in 5 degree weather with winds blowing over twenty miles per hour.

Governor Carey was also concerned that some people might freeze in the cold without transportation. At an Albany press conference he blamed the LPOOC, saying they had been in charge. State officials and the LPOOC staff sniped at each other. State staff said they had helped design the plan, but the LPOOC did not follow it. LPOOC officials responded that the state had been involved every step of the way and knew what was going on.

It was not as if committee officials were not aware there could be problems. In fact, in the days before the games, there had been concern about the lack of buses and drivers. The LPOOC had arranged for buses to be available from Rive Sud, a Quebec Company. That company had subcontracts with other bus lines but did not have all the buses Lake Placid needed. Union officials also complained about using Canadian drivers, so a decision was made to put US drivers on the buses.

State Transportation Commissioner William Henessey asked Governor Carey to declare a limited state of emergency after a heavy snowfall clogged the roads. This declaration allowed the state to contract with bus companies without normal bidding procedures and to authorize longer work hours than usually allowed by law. The state also asked for school buses from school districts all around the Olympic region and arranged for buses from the Fugazy Travel of New Jersey and other private bus lines.

DEC Commissioner Robert Flacke took command of the state response. He said he found there had been "no communication and no management at all." Working with Greyhound executives, state transportation staff, and LPOOC staff, a management plan had been developed within six to seven hours to parcel out responsibilities. He added that "over a twenty hour period, they had developed an effective transportation system since Day 3." The plan finally began to work and the situation dramatically improved by Sunday and Monday. There were 378 buses running by Sunday, including 46 school buses that carried 342,000 total riders. Flacke said the real heroes were the state employees working with him and the LPOOC who executed a new transportation system and pulled the games from the brink of chaos. His team included Roy Torkelson, Richard Persico and Peter Lanahan and Victor Gleider.

The *Washington Post* reported in its Sunday edition on February 17, "The most confusing question during the first week of the Winter Olympics has not been who would win which medal. It has been the task of deciding whether these Games are a lovely, snowy, slow-paced winter carnival or the most incredibly botched boondoggle and ripoff imaginable."

The uproar and crisis subsided and finally the entire focus of the games was on the athletic competition. As the second week of the games opened, the atmosphere was more relaxed and more carnival-like. The weather turned mild and shops reported a big increase in visitors. The trading of Olympic pins became a collectible phenomenon at the games for the first time as athletes and visitors from all over the world exchanged pins from their home countries.

The *Washington Post* reported that the mood was "remarkably jolly." "Walk the streets at night and you are in the midst of some Dickensian idyll about Christmases past. The Adirondack scenery, after a foot of fresh snow in the last four days, is as gorgeous as any postcard imaginable."

When I arrived on Monday for the day to watch the ski jump competition, it was clear and cold, only about 10 degrees but I was dressed for it. I later wrote in my journal,

"It was a town filled with color. There are national and Olympic flags gracing the sports facilities and venues. Banners hung on Main Street and the visitors were garbed in the bright colors of winter sports clothing. The crowd was definitely not poor. 35 mm cameras hung around the necks of many.

Lake Placid had changed in appearance since I had last spent time there a year and a half earlier. I felt like I was going back to a house I once lived in. Its sight was familiar and brought memories but it was different. The old quaint exteriors of some of the buildings had been modernized. Others were gone like the quaint Homestead Inn on a hill which gave way for the new concrete Hilton Hotel built into the hill which dominated the corner of Main Street and Saranac Avenue.

I am glad I went. I wanted to be there. The huge crowds were a hassle in that it was hard to relax. It was fun but I could never have stayed

for much longer without having a place to get away from it all. The movie theater on Main Street provided that refuge for one person I saw interviewed on television. In fact, that one theater on Main Street would have been a movie lover's paradise. Each day it offered about six recent movies."

Main Street in Lake Placid, Monday afternoon, February 18, 1980 (author photo)

Meanwhile, Eric Heiden was continuing his own great drama. On that Monday, Eric Heiden won his third gold medal in the 1000 meter race, having to fight through 35 mile per hour winds but still setting an Olympic record. His three gold medals equaled the most for an entire American team since the 1952 Olympics.

On Thursday, despite his skate sticking in the ice on a turn, Heiden recovered to break the Olympic record and win the 1500 meter race for his fourth gold medal. He was heading into the weekend with one last race. He had broken the Olympic record in all four performances and the world record twice.

Sweden's Ingemar Stenmark won the giant slalom race, which was witnessed by young King Carl XVI Gustav and Queen Silvia who had come to attend the games. They were great sports enthusiasts who had met at the Munich games when Gustav was still a prince. When Gustav's father died in 1974, he became King. Gustav and Sofia were at the top of the hill to watch Stenmark and then they rolled down the snowy hill to get to the bottom.

As Wednesday, February 20th came, President Carter re-affirmed that since his ultimatum of a month earlier had passed with no adequate response from the Soviets, the United States would boycott the Moscow games or seek to have them moved. If that failed, the US would organize alternate games for boycotting countries.

Mike Eruzione said the US hockey team was only focused on its games and was not mingling and enjoying the atmosphere on the street. They stayed only with teammates and family during the games, especially as the team kept winning and getting more publicity. He and his teammates were able to unwind at the "hostage house," a joking reference to the international situation in Iran. That was a house next to the arena on the hill where his parents and parents of the other players were staying together. He said he was amazed at how close all the families became while staying there and experiencing the drama and excitement of their sons playing for an Olympic medal.

On Wednesday, as the USA was beating West Germany, 4-2, the Soviet team remained undefeated by beating Canada. Now it was clear the two were going to face each other in the semifinals, just two days after President Carter said the United States would boycott the summer games in Moscow.

Chapter Eleven

A Sound that Reverberated Around the Mountains

"It was the right team in the right place at the right time in the only head-to-head physical and emotional US-USSR confrontation this side of the Persian Gulf."

—Peter Gammons, Boston Globe

Sometimes it takes a sporting event, such as a World Series or playoff series, a little while to gain its story line and the same could be said of the 1980 Olympic Games. As fans watched at home night after night, they became more interested in the games, learning more about the athletes and the competition. For the United States, the competition against the Soviets drew much heightened interest because of the international crisis and the threat of the United States to boycott the Summer games. Little did the Americans watching the games know just days earlier that what they would see on that Friday night would be a moment of magic and joy that would produce iconic images for decades to come.

A sense of excitement and tension about the hockey showdown between the United States and Soviet Union built as Friday approached. While the US team had a chance, few thought it had much of a chance. After all, they had just played the Soviets two nights before the Olympic competition and they were manhandled, 10-3 at Madison Square Garden. The Soviet teams had won the hockey gold medal in the four preceding Olympics in 1964, 1968, 1972 and 1976 and had only lost once one game in Olympic competition since 1968. They had some of the greatest players in the world and had beaten NHL teams in tournaments during those years.

US Coach Herb Brooks who had been so hard on his players psyched up his team in the locker room before the game, telling them this was their moment. According to the coach's biography by John Gilbert, Brooks joked before the game, "If Tikhonov (the Soviet coach) loses, he goes to Siberia. I we lose, I go back to St. Paul."

The semifinal game was played at 5:00 o'clock Eastern Standard Time. ABC had wanted to change the time of the game and broadcast it live in the evening across the United States but its agreement with the LPOOC only allowed a change in times if all parties agreed. ABC even agreed to pay an additional $125,000 to do so, according to Jim Spence who was Executive Vice Persident under Roone Arledge. The Soviets did not agree. The game would be able to be seen at midnight in Moscow if it was kept at its planned 5:00 p.m. time rather than in the middle of the night if the game was played later to accommodate American viewers. So, ABC had to show the game on a tape delay in the evening to allow more to see it. Canadian television showed the game live and many along the US border in New York and other states were able to watch the Canadian broadcast as the game was played and they knew the result before it was shown in the United States.

Thirty-four million American households tuned in to see the game with more watching in bars and public places across the country. ABC's Jim McKay, who was reporting live at the beginning of the game, would not announce the outcome. However, viewers like me had a feeling something dramatic might have happened because the crowd shown outside the arena was filled with revelers.

The arena which was built to hold 8500 had 11,000 people in it. Vice President Walter Mondale and his wife, Joan, were there sitting with Petr Spurney. Eric Heiden and many other American athletes were there. Greg McConnell and Olympic staff were there.

It was a close, tense game. The Soviets seemed in control though and outshot the US team, 38-16. The United States team was behind early in the game, but every time it seemed the game was getting out of hand for them, they came back. They tied the score twice and then Captain Mike Eruzione would score the game winner in the final period. Those who followed the winter games know the story and might even have seen the final seconds of the game played over and over again to ABC announcer Al Michael's query, "Do you believe in miracles?" The players threw their sticks in the air and rushed Jim Craig. The Soviets stood silently

**USA hockey team on the podium after receiving gold medals
(Lake Placid Olympic Museum photo)**

and watched. Everyone who was there mentions how the noise in the arena was deafening said the building seemed to shake as the crowd let out a chant, "USA, USA, USA."

McKay, in the anchor seat, would say that, in all his decades of broadcasting sports, this was the greatest moment he had ever covered. What is it if not "something not so wonderfully pure about it all."

LPOOC staff member Greg McConnell was trying to escort the White House press corps to their van outside the arena. He took them down a back stairway. The two hockey teams were on their way to their dressing rooms. The US team was euphoric and excited and the Soviet team was like "nothing," said McConnell. The dejection was all consuming. As he escorted the press outside he opened the "panic" door and saw a huge crowd and the press van at a 30 degree angle.

Spectators emptied into Main Street as car horns blared and church bells chimed. The crowd kept chanting, "USA, USA, USA." The Main Street Liquor store sold out of champagne and closed. At Mr. Mike's Pizza, which was two blocks away on Main Street, owner Dave Nicola said the noise from the arena could be heard inside his restaurant. That night and the next would be the two best nights in the history of his business even to this day. Janey Sorensen, who was working in a photo booth on Main Street told public television thirty years later, "I can't explain the joy. This was my little town that I had grown up in."

Ed Stransenback, the LPOOC press service director, watched the last two periods from the press box. He felt the building literally "bouncing" during the last ten minutes of the game when the roar of the crowd was "deafening." After the game he helped with the hockey team's press conference, which had 900 media attending. He said that Norwegian journalists went to the TASS press office and found that the Soviet reporters had closed the door and the window shades.

Dr. Paul Reiss, who grew up in Lake Placid said, "In the context of the times, it didn't matter whether it was a hockey game...it was the United States against the Soviet Union." He said the sound of cheering from the arena was so loud it "reverberated around the mountains."

Jim Plummer and John Furey of the Albany area were pictured celebrating outside the arena on the front page of the *Knickerbocker News* the next day. Jim said he has seen a lot of great football games at the old Giants stadium "but nothing compared to the intensity of that game." He and John were sitting behind the Soviet goalie in the third period and as the game ended they glanced at Soviet coach Tikhonov, looked at each other, and said, "he's fired."

Anthony Pitkiewicz of Albany was one of ten van drivers for New York Telephone Company who had permits to shuttle their employees to their worksite in the village. He was on his way down Main Street to pick up operators from the central office when the game ended and a huge crowd emptied into the street. He had to inch his way along the street. "It was just like Times Square on New Year's Eve," he said with all the people and the cheering and the noise.

My cousin, Beth Portolese, who was working in Lake Placid at the time, did not attend the game but said the entire small town was able to take part in the celebration on the street and in the hotels, mingling with media and athletes from around the world. It was that atmosphere that made the Lake Placid games so unique for the residents and spectators.

The *New York Times* reported the next day, "Car horns blared, bells jangled, fireworks crackled and shrieks of joy reverberated across the nation." Let them have Afghanistan, one man shouted. We've got the gold." Strangers in bars embraced and sang "God Bless America."

Time magazine noted, "At a Stop and Shop supermarket in Cambridge Massachusetts, a p.a system suddenly blurted that the US hockey team had beaten the Soviets. The store erupted as bags of cookies, paper towels and anything else handy were tossed into the air with pandemonious cheering. Seventy people gathered outside Mike Eruzione's house in Winthrop, Massachusetts and sang the national anthem. One psychiatrist reported his patients' telling him how, for days, tears shot to their eyes when they thought of those Americans boys."

Sports Illustrated reported that several drivers pulled off the road and honked their horns while listening to their car radios. Then they got out of their cars and started screaming and celebrating in the rain.

Vice President Walter Mondale had returned for the game and he reflected,

"I was thrilled when we won. There was a special Minnesota aspect because of the coach and many of the players as well...The enthusiasm and glory of the moment was unforgettable. Joan was with me and we still talk about it...Even though, as Vice President, I was quite well known, the public reaction at the Olympics was incredible. Everybody must have been watching."

President Jimmy Carter said it was "a very emotional moment" and he wrote in his diary

I immediately called the coach, Herb Brooks, congratulated them, and invited the team to the White House Monday. He responded that he strongly supported our not attending the Moscow Olympics in the summer.

The Soviet Tass news agency attributed the defeat to mistakes by defensive players and goalies and "elements of confusion and a lack of concentration." The Soviet team had one more game on Sunday and beat Sweden to win the silver medal. They never sent their medals back to be inscribed after the games.

To those who were not following the competition in detail, the win might have seemed like the US had won the gold medal. But the team had only won the semifinal game. To win the gold, they had to play again on Sunday morning, the last day of competition, against Finland. It was another game watched by millions of Americans and the US team again went behind early. You had a feeling though that this deficit probably would not stand either. And it did not. The US team came back to win, 4-2. As the game came to a jubilant end, Al Michaels proclaimed, "The impossible dream has come true!"

The whole team rushed onto the ice. Goalie Jim Craig, wrapped in the American flag, skated on the ice as he looked for his father. That was one of the most remembered images of the moment and one of the most iconic American images of the generation.

Once again, euphoria erupted around the country. At Radio City Music Hall in New York, the crowd spontaneously began singing The Star-Spangled Banner when the result was announced. The victory seemed like a giant catharsis for the United States. It was not just the "thrill of victory," or that it was a defeat of the Soviets.

Some said it was the greatest thing since the moon landing a little over a decade earlier. An older person compared it to another very political Olympic moment when American Jesse Owens won in track at the Berlin Olympics in 1936 to challenge Hitler's advocacy of Aryan supremacy.

A little while later the hockey team's gold medal ceremony was a scene made for a movie. All the players received their medals and came onto the podium together. It was a moment of sheer innocence and joy that swept away for the moment all the frustration about hostages and boycotts. Grown men admitted to having lumps in their throats or even crying because what they had seen was the best of American youth with an enthusiasm that somehow seemed to be typically American.

Lance Morrow wrote in a *Time* magazine essay, "It would be a mistake to exaggerate the significance of the joyful outburst; in a tough winter for American morale, the Olympic hockey was a lovely diversion. Still, the moment was connected in some deeper ways to the emergence of a new patriotic impulse in America." How ironic that such patriotism would take place in Lake Placid, which was also the home of Kate Smith. Miss Smith not only made "God Bless America" her theme song, but she was also a hockey fan adopted by the Philadelphia Flyers NHL team as a good luck charm when she sang before their games.

Boston Globe writer Peter Gammons even asked the then curse-stricken Boston Red Sox to take note that the US hockey team won with "consummate character, a team playing the toughest and the best in the stretch of every close game."

Mike Eruzione was asked by reporters about the victory and he quoted his teammate Phil Verchota, "We're all a bunch of big doolies now." "It just means big wheel, big gun, big shot," Verchota who had coined the term explained. That was the headline in Dave Anderson's *New York Times* column.

Eric Heiden was at the big game, screaming for his American teammates and celebrating afterward. Then, he slept late, skipped breakfast but was so motivated by the hockey game he defied those who wondered if he could win a longer race, taking the 10,000 meter race with thousands of fans cheering him on in the bleachers and the adjoining street. Not since Irving Jaffee in Lake Placid in 1932 had an American won the 10,000 meter race. Heiden's fifth gold medal would earn him the recognition as the "world's outstanding male athlete" of 1980 and he would win the Sullivan Award as America's outstanding amateur athlete.

Heiden shunned the publicity though, "I just want to be Eric Heiden, I don't want people to put me on a pedestal." He was more interested in the personal challenge of racing, saying "It really doesn't matter whether I win or lose as long as I do my best." He said he did not want to be like 1976 decathlon winner Bruce Jenner and have his face on a box of Wheaties.

In Lake Placid, "an air of conviviality" broke out after the hockey win, said Sallie Warner, a native of the village and daughter of Favor Smith, who had been one of the town leaders and member of the LPOOC. She watched Eric Heiden win his gold medals and wished there had been "a little more balance" in the attention given his performances and the hockey win.

The US teams won 12 medals at the games, all but Phil Mahre's skiing silver medal were won in skating events. Beth Heiden won the bronze in the 3000 meter speed skating race. Leah Mueller won two silver medals in speed skating. Linda Fratiane won a silver medal in figure skating. Many thought she should have won the gold but lost to East Germany's Annett Poetsch. Charles Tickner won a bronze in figure skating and of course, the hockey team won the gold. The East Germans won 23 medals. The Soviet Union finished second with 22 medals, including 10 gold medals.

The whole country seemed on a high as the Winter Games ended in Lake Placid on February 24th in the Olympic arena. Rochester's Chuck Mangione played his original song, "Give it All You've Got," written for the games. Lord Killanin at the closing ceremonies said the Lake Placid games "proved we can do something to improve the mutual understanding of the world. He received a long ovation when he added, "If we could all come together, it would be for a better world if we can avoid the holocaust which may well be upon us if we are not careful."

The day after the games a large crowd on the South lawn of the White House cheered as President Carter welcomed the team and hugged Eric Heiden and others. Heiden had planned to deliver a petition to the White House with the names of most of the US athletes, expressing opposition to the boycott of the summer games and what that would mean for the athletes, but there had not been an opportunity to do so. The following week, a letter signed by 61 members of the USA Olympics team was sent to the President urging him to find a way for American athletes to participate in Moscow. The letter said:

"Mr. President, we urge you to use your most prestigious office to try to assure that our fellow athletes, who have trained diligently for the Olympic Summer Games, are provided the same opportunity that we have just experienced by participating in the Winter Games. We can all assure you that there is no substitute for participation in the Olympics. We all agree that the Olympic games represent the highlight of our athletic careers."

Some like goalie Jim Craig and Coach Herb Brooks were in support of the President's stance though.

**President Carter at the White House with US team
February 25, 1980 (Lake Placid Olympic Museum photo)**

Eric Heiden, writing about the boycott of the Moscow games in the *New York Times* in 1988 before the Calgary Games, reflected,

"Only a few careers can span two Olympics and to think that with the stroke of a pen, a politician can ruin that one chance for an athlete is horrifying."

He went on about the boycott, "During the 1980 Winter Games, President Carter decided to boycott the Summer Games. Very few people, including me, understood the extent to which the boycott destroyed the opportunities and dreams of so many athletes. Now, I'm sorry I didn't do more to fight the boycott."

While the USOC said it would abide by Carter's wishes, it did not make a final decision until its April meeting in Colorado Springs, again coming under heavy pressure from the Carter Administration. The meeting was deemed so important by the administration that Vice President Walter Mondale flew to Colorado and spoke about the importance of the supporting the country. He expressed his sense of the pain the athletes felt and understood the special moment of participating in the Olympics, saying, "Few moments in my life match the electricity I felt at Lake Placid."

In the Vice President's speech to the IOC, he quoted Ernest Jahncke, an American member of the IOC, who wanted to boycott the Berlin Olympics in 1936. Jahncke said, "If our committee permits the games to be held in Germany, there will be nothing left to distinguish the Olympic idea from the Nazi ideal."

The USOC had wanted to be ready for athletes to attend just in case there was some last minute compromise or action that would clear the way for the US to attend. There were still many who were not happy about the boycott and they were resisting it. Some of the athletes made a counterproposal that would permit the athletes to go to Moscow, but not participate in the opening and closing ceremonies and limit their public presence outside their own competitive events.

In the end, though, the cost of going against the White House was too much for the Olympic committee. They ran the risk of going against public opinion and being accused of being unpatriotic. It was clear that the Carter Administration intended to use whatever legal means it could to stop athletes from going to Moscow and pressure was brought to bear on corporate sponsors of the USOC. Sears Roebuck withheld a contribution of $25,000 to the USOC unless the committee supported the White House. Without corporate and governmental support, the USOC would face a major financial crisis. In the end, the USOC voted to support the boycott by a 2 to 1 margin and tried to leverage their vote for government financial support for the USOC and for the summer games coming in Los Angeles in 1984. Lake Placid's Serge Lussi, a member of USOC, voted against the boycott.

A group of 25 athletes sued the USOC for violating its constitution, which said a committee could only withdraw for sports-related reasons. The class action suit sought an injunction, saying the USOC backed down to political pressure. They lost with a judge ruling the USOC voted independently despite government advocacy for the boycott.

"Viewed through the prism of international history, you tend to forget that there were people hurt by this decision, hundreds of athletes, torn between supporting their president in an international crisis even as they wondered how their lifetime dream had been shattered by an invasion on the other side of the world." wrote Christine Brennan in *USA Today*, twenty five years later.

After the vote by the IOC, Britain's Prime Minister Margaret Thatcher strongly supported the boycott but the British Olympic Association voted to participate in Moscow. Some other countries that boycotted the games also allowed their athletes to go to Moscow on their own or to participate as a member of another country if they had dual citizenship. Many of those athletes went to Moscow and marched into the opening ceremonies under the Olympic flag.

In Moscow, as the games opened in July, Lord Killanin was ending his tenure as IOC President. He directly criticized President
Carter's decision stating, "I personally think it's unfortunate that
the President of the United States, on sporting matters, was not
fully informed of the facts...They did not understand how sport is
organized in the world. They did not understand how national
Olympic committees work. They did not understand the work-
ings of the International Olympic Committee."

The United States led a boycott of 64 countries choosing not to
participate in Moscow. An alternate games were planned and
Petr Spurney was called in for advice. In July, the US sponsored
the Liberty Bell Classic Games for boycotting countries and 28
nations came to Philadelphia to take part.

In retaliation, on May 8, 1984 the Soviet Union, East Germany
and thirteen other countries announced a boycott of the 1984
Summer Games in Los Angeles and hosted their own alternate
Friendship games. Other countries joining the Soviet boycott in
addition to East Germany were countries in the Warsaw Pact and
politically aligned with the Soviet Union: Poland, Hungary,
Czechoslovakia, Bulgaria and Laos, Mongolia, Cuba, South
Yemen, North Korea, Vietnam, Afghanistan and Angola.

US and Soviet athletes would go for a twelve year span, beginning with the games in Montreal in 1976 to those in Seoul in
1988, before competing in the Summer Olympics. Other than
the political pressure the boycott did not change the Soviets military plans. Their government and press blamed the United
States hostility for the boycott. The Soviets stayed in
Afghanistan for nine more years.

As for Heiden, he would race the weekend after the Olympics in
front of 20,000 people in Heerenveen, the Netherlands and lose
his world championship title, finishing second to a Dutchman,
Hilbert ver der Duim. He seemed relieved that he was taken off

his pedestal. He told the *New York Times*, "It wasn't that disagreeable to have everyone think of you as perfect, but it's going to be easier to do without it. I really wanted to win, but was very tough to be up mentally here and I'm really looking forward to doing other things." He would race again later in the month of March and then he retired from skating and set out on a career in cycling and finishing his medical degree. He was the doctor for the USA team at the 2010 winter games in Vancouver.

The day after the Olympics ended, the streets of Lake Placid were quiet again and the village, which had been the stage for a great drama, was now like an empty theater with only the maintenance personnel and employees still around to clean up. Petr Spurney dispatched Greg McConnell to go "lock down" the Olympic village because some of the valuable, donated merchandise like hot tubs and televisions were disappearing. The committee was in debt and needed to get everything inventoried and then sold at auction. Soon, the committee staff would be dramatically downsized because they were broke.

Some in town might have been relieved but there was a great emotional letdown after more than five years of planning and anticipation. There was also an overwhelming pride and thrill that the village had become world famous for hosting what was then the greatest American Olympics of them all. After the games were over, the extent of that fame was clear. The Lake Placid Olympics were, at that time, the most watched winter games in US history with 170 of the nation's 220 million people viewing part of the games. It turned out that the biggest audience was not for the hockey games, but for the women's figure skating championship on the last evening of competition. The people of Lake Placid might have been let down when it was over but Lake Placid's place in Olympic and national history was forever sealed.

Chapter Twelve
Aftermath

"In two weeks people will forget about the buses, the prices, the commercialization, the worst I have ever seen. They will think of Lake Placid and get a tear in their eyes."

—Serge Lange, French reporter

W hat happened in Lake Placid in February 1980 could never happen again: a small mountain town hosting the Winter Olympics in an intimate setting with the story of the games written by amateur collegians who just came together to play hockey and skate.

In his foreword to Wayne Coffey's book, *The Boys of Winter*, goalie Jim Craig said, "I've visited quite a few places that have hosted the Olympics in the past, and you almost can't tell that the Games were ever there. You aren't in Lake Placid more than a minute before you are flooded with Olympic memories, whether it's from seeing the Olympic Arena at the top of the hill or the oval next door where Heiden skated into immortality."

The 1980 Winter Olympics will always be remembered for the "Miracle on Ice" and the great feats of Eric Heiden. The afterglow has lit the fortunes of Lake Placid ever since. Movies and books have been made about the *"Miracle"* at Lake Placid.

The hockey team were named "Sportsmen of the Year" by *Sports Illustrated* magazine. The magazine also called the hockey win over the Soviet Union the greatest sports moment of the 20th century. Fourteen members of the hockey team went on to have careers in the National Hockey League.

The Soviet Union's hockey team would go on to win the gold medal in the next five Winter Olympics and lose only once, making the US win at Lake Placid all the more remarkable and unique.

Less than ten years after the Lake Placid games, the Berlin Wall fell and Communism collapsed in Eastern Europe. In 1991, the Soviet Union was dissolved into fifteen separate nations with Russia being the largest. In the years after the games, Jim Rogers has been a tour guide at the Olympic Arena. Many times there were Russians tourists who wanted to see the arena and as they walked around they agreed with Jim that "this is not where Communism fell, but it is where the slide began."

In assessing the staging of the games, the Lake Placid organizing committee was sarcastically called the "disorganizing committee." An Italian journalist told the *Toronto Globe and Mail* that the games were the "second worst organized event he had covered, only ranking behind the Second World War."

Serge Lange, a correspondent for a French sports paper, assailed the transportation, the press facilities and the distance of the accommodations, telling the *Washington Post* they were a "zero." He went on to say the sports events were outstanding and that people will have fond and emotional memories of the games at Lake Placid.

That may be the case, especially for the Baby Boomer Americans like me. Those games were a highlight of our youth. I remember feeling such a sense of pride and happiness after the games ended. In Lake Placid where there had been so much controversy before the games, there was a feeling of relief that life could return to normal but there was also a letdown. It was like having a spectacular dream and waking up and looking around and finding everything the way it was before. In reality, what had changed was that most were exhilarated by the experience and took great pride that the dramatic events had happened in Lake Placid. The Olympics made history and brought unprecedented fame and attention to the village. There were few who expressed regret about the town hosting the Olympics.

Lise Bang Jensen covered the games for Albany's now defunct *Knickerbocker News*. She said that the Lake Placid was a "charming" place for the games to be held because it felt like such a real community in a small town environment, not the overdone, super-hyped extravaganzas now held in urban areas. To Pat Corbett of Rome, New York, who was working in the National Guard driving trucks during the games, there was a "romance" about Lake Placid.

To Petr Spurney, the Lake Placid games were the "last Olympics that demonstrated the full impact of the amateur side." He felt that because of the Miracle on Ice, the winter Olympics took off. Four years later in Sarajevo ABC spent $96 million for the television rights to the games. He regretted that the games ended with a deficit. Despite unexpected expenses like having to pay for the constant cost of snow making due to the mild winter, they had been on target to break even until the extra costs for the buses.

The Winter Olympics will almost certainly not return to Lake Placid a third time. The games are too big now for a small town like Lake Placid. Turin, Italy hosted the games in 2006 and was the largest city at the time to hold the games with a population of 900,000. Then, in 2010, Vancouver, a larger city played host. In

2014 the athletes will gather in Sochi, Russia, a city of nearly 350,000 on the Black Sea and in 2018, the city of Pyeonchang in South Korea will have the honor.

For better or worse, the Winter Olympics have become the opposite of what Lake Placid's organizers had in mind when they sought "an Olympics in perspective." They wanted to focus on the amateur athletic competition. Indeed, the IOC's original quaint notion of the games to glorify the athletic competition has changed too. The games of the 21st century are a corporate-backed, media extravaganza for professional athletes anchored in a large city but spread over a region with budgets of over a billion dollars. The number of sports for which medals are awarded jumped to 77 in Vancouver in 2010.

The Lake Placid organizers' notion that the games were for the athletes not the spectators seemed naive even in 1980. Now, the competition would not be possible without the corporate sponsors to pay for televising to a worldwide audience. Lake Placid 1980 is like the Original Six teams of the NHL versus the 30 team league of today.

In 1986, the IOC changed its charter to allow "all the world's great male and female athletes to participate." It was not until 1998 though that the National Hockey League finally allowed its stars to compete for the first time at the Nagano games. There are no more Boston University Terriers and Minnesota Gophers amateurs on the US team. Now, it is the stars of the NHL representing their home countries. While the sense of an underdog collegian's excitement is no longer, the 2010 Olympic hockey gold medal contest in Vancouver between the United States and Canadian teams of NHL players produced intense interest in hockey-mad Canada and the largest hockey viewership in the United States since the Lake Placid games. The victory for the home team Canadians was a special moment of national pride and excitement.

When the winter games returned to the United States in 2002 in Salt Lake, the cost was $1.9 billion, over ten times the actual cost and more than five times the inflation-adjusted total cost at Lake Placid. With all the corporate sponsorship and television rights, the Salt Lake committee had a $40 million surplus. There were 77 events and more than 2500 athletes participating in 78 events. Taking place just five months after September 11, 2001, security alone in Salt Lake cost $240 million. That was more than the entire games in Lake Placid.

Corporate sponsorship had also exploded and Salt Lake's games were mired in controversy with the effort of some of its organizing committee members to offer expensive gifts to IOC members who would vote on the bids for those games. Perks included college tuition payments for some family members of IOC officials. Several of the IOC members were forced to resign along with the leaders of the Salt Lake Organizing Committee.

Businessman Mitt Romney was brought in to take over and clean up the mess and embarrassment of the Salt Lake City committee. The games were successful though and one of the great moments for the US team was the gold medal victory in the skeleton race of young Jimmy Shea, grandson of Jack, who had won a gold medal in Lake Placid 70 years earlier. Jim's father, Jim Shea, Sr., and a member of the 1964 US team joined him at the Salt Lake games. Sadly Jack, 91, was killed by a drunk driver in a crash in Lake Placid, just seventeen days before the start of the Salt Lake games, which he planned to attend.

In September 1980, less than eight months after the Lake Placid Olympics, the athletes' village had been renovated and opened as a medium security prison. A ceremony was held by state and local officials. Rev. Graham Hodges from Watertown, Jonathan Gradess, an activist in criminal justice issues and five other protesters from STOP stood in the rain holding banners.

Lake Placid gained a permanent role for itself in the US Olympic movement when the USOC designated it along with Colorado Springs, Colorado and Chula Vista, California as one of three official training sites for athletes preparing for the Olympics. In 1982, the training center was opened. A new facility with 96 private rooms was built and opened in 1989. Athletes now come to Lake Placid or live there and train year round. The US luge and bobsled associations have their headquarters in Lake Placid.

Just as many predicted, the LPOOC ended up with a debt. It was less than $10 million, which was nothing compared to losses for Montreal and other host cities. In a report on US funding for Olympic games in 2001, the General Accounting Office estimated the "total direct costs to plan and stage" the Lake Placid games at $363 million in 2001 dollars when all the supporting costs of federal agencies were included, not just the outlays for administration and construction. The report noted that the federal share of the costs at Lake Placid was about 50% while it was only 18% at Salt Lake City with more corporate money raised. The report noted that most of the federal money in Lake Placid was for construction of facilities but in later years, the bulk of the federal expenses would be for security costs.

The LPOOC stayed in operation for several years as it worked to pay off debts and complete its business, which included rebuilding the high school athletic fields. Two years after the games, the *New York Times* reported that the committee put 620 checks in the mail totaling $8.2 million to pay debts.

To satisfy the debt issues and the maintenance and use of the Olympic facilities, legislation was passed by the New York State Legislature in 1981 authorizing the state to purchase facilities that would be operated by the new Olympic Regional Development Authority (ORDA) in 1981. The State Urban Development Corporation (UDC) purchased them and then transferred ownership to the Town of North Elba which would lease them back to ORDA to manage beginning in April 1982. ORDA also had access to funds from the 1979 New York State Olympic Lottery.

In its early years, ORDA was run by Ned Harkness, championship winning college and NHL hockey coach. ORDA has hosted over 350 major national and international competitions since it began. It has promoted tourism of the bobsled and luge runs and promotes concerts and sports events at the 1980 Arena. That arena and the 1932 arena were renamed to honor Herb Brooks and Jack Shea.

Ironically both of these greats died in tragic car accidents. Herb Brooks fell asleep while driving in Minnesota in 2003, a year after Shea's death. The ski jump complex is named after Ron MacKenzie and also has a statue of Art Devlin. The Olympic torch platform has been named after Rev. Bernard Fell.

(In 2010, New York Governor David Paterson went to the Olympic Museum in Lake Placid and signed "Shea's law." This law allows blood samples taken by certified nursing assistants and emergency medical technicians without doctor supervision to be admitted as evidence in drunk driving cases. Those samples were suppressed in the Shea case and charges against the drunk driver were dismissed).

The arena has become "hallowed ground" in the hockey world, a sacred sports site. In 2011, the Boston Bruins lost the first two games at home of the opening Stanley Cup quarterfinals against the Montreal Canadiens. They won the next game in Montreal and then had two nights off before game four. So, rather than stay in Montreal or return to Boston, they decided to travel the two hours to Lake Placid and practice on the Olympic ice. The Bruins left inspired and they returned to beat Montreal in game four and win the series in seven games. They then won three more series including two game sevens to win their first Stanley Cup since 1972!

Lake Placid has become a town for athletes of all types and, in the past few decades, it has not only hosted the traditional winter sports competition and the Empire State Winter Games, but it has become host for numerous other competitions. Some of these include the Goodwill Games in 2000, an annual half marathon race, a bike race and the Ironman competition, all of which bring thousands to the town and region. It continues to have its skating training sessions and ice shows in the summer along with hockey competition.

The Olympic hockey victory in 1980 led to an explosion of interest in hockey by young Americans. Before that there were few American-born players in the National Hockey League. However, that has changed and the US Olympic team of American-born players went to the finals in the 2010 games in Vancouver and will be a medal contender in the future as well.

A Winter Olympics Museum opened in the new Olympic Arena in 1994 and houses many trophies, uniforms, medals and photos and banners from the Winter Olympics through the years.

Even though development is controlled in the Adirondack Park, Lake Placid has become an upscale community in the last thirty years with several condo developments built in the village along with some very exclusive lodges and timeshare units.

Business has grown so much that most local retailers say there are very few times now that there is an "off-season." Associations hold annual meetings in the fall. Athletes train all year and tourists continue to come, even though the village has not been immune to the havoc caused by the Great Recession in the last few years. The Olympics though did what the North Country boys had hoped by strengthening the local economy of Lake Placid and maintaining the environment and the charm of the village.

There had even been talk of bidding again for the Winter Olympics though possible plans were to join with other nearby cities like Albany or Montreal because the games have grown so large. It is now unquestioned that Lake Placid could never accommodate them. Former New York Governor George Pataki created a task force to explore the possibility of two nation games with Quebec and Lake Placid but nothing has come of it. Serge Lussi thinks the Montreal-Lake Placid partnership would be a very appealing one but he said the IOC and USOC are not enthusiastic. They don't think a two-nation plan would work.

It may be that the games can never again be held in a small town. NBC is spending $775 million on the television rights to cover the 2014 games in Sochi, Russia. It is paying a combined total of $4.38 billion for the rights at Sochi, the summer games in Rio in 2016, the winter games in South Korea in 2018 and the summer games at an undetermined site in 2020.

Ironically, now forty years after withdrawing from the Olympics, Denver has begun thinking about a bid for the 2022 winter games. Inquiries have been made of the IOC to determine if there is any lasting enmity for being the only host community which withdrew after being awarded the games. A committee has been formed and has determined the games would cost $1.5 billion.

In the years since the 1980 games, Lake Placid has celebrated the major anniversaries of that time. Most of the hockey players returned in 2005 for the 25th anniversary and re-naming of the arena as the Herb Brooks Arena. There were big celebrations and festivals to mark the games with the restoration of the torch and re-lighting of it at the 25th anniversary in 2005 when a weeklong celebration was held and again in 2010. Jim Craig returned for the 25th anniversary and lit the torch. Mike Eruzione said he has been back to Lake Placid about twenty-five times including taking his son to participate in a Can-Am hockey tournament.

Though the games will probably never return to Lake Placid, the athletes from the village and the spirit of Lake Placid keep returning to the Olympics. No town or city except Lake Placid has sent athletes to every Winter Olympic Games and no town sends as many athletes to the winter games as Lake Placid. In Vancouver in 2010, the flag bearer for the United States was Bill Grimmette at his fifth Olympic games. Andrew Weibrecht of Lake Placid won the bronze in the Giant slalom, Bill Demong of Vernmontville won the gold in the Nordic combined. The spirit of the 1980 Olympics remains and the legacy continues to make Lake Placid the winter sports capital of the nation if not the world - just what the North Country Boys wanted and felt the community deserved.

Acknowledgements

W hen I started working on this book, I wondered if the whole story of the 1980 Winter Olympics had already been told. There have been movies about the "Miracle on Ice" and a video production about Lake Placid's Olympic history. I realized, though, that while many who lived in Lake Placid or worked at the games may have known the events leading up to the games, there were so many details that a movie could not report and so many interesting stories to these games that needed to be told.

I had forgotten until I was looking through a lot of old files that I had actually inquired about working at the 1980 Olympics. I received a letter from the LPOOC acknowledging my interest though no job materialized. I collected a lot of memorabilia during the games, and continue to collect many items including at least a dozen original posters as well as medallions, programs for the opening and closing ceremonies, post cards, mugs, playing cards and books.

I kept copies of the *Albany Times Union* and now defunct *Knicker-bocker News* and the *Watertown Daily Times* from during the Olympic Games as well as some clippings from before and after. I was aware of the controversy about the "Olympic Prison" and was on a list from some of those opposed to the prison. I received stacks of clippings with hundreds of articles about the prison issue and the Olympics. I also had two of the famed posters from the group STOP (Stop the Olympic Prison) which was the subject of a lawsuit after the United States Olympic Committee demanded that the depiction of jail bars touching the Olympic rings be withdrawn because of trademark infringement. Those have all been valuable in my research for this book.

I have been able to find a lot of videos on YouTube of the actual coverage of the 1980 games, which was rare. There are many personal VCR recordings on You Tube. I watched the ABC Sports VHS video of the highlights of the games.

A number of people who were involved in the planning of the games were very willing to discuss their experiences. These included Jim Rogers and Serge Lussi who were on the LPOOC. General Manager, Petr Spurney, provided great insight into the background of the games and the struggles and planning. Counsel Bill Kissel, Greg McConnell, and Ed Stransanback provided information on their experiences working on the professional staff for the years leading up to and including the games. Former New York State officials including Mark Lawton and Robert Flacke provided invaluable insight into the state's role in the management of the games. Robert Flacke was on the ground during the games and worked closely with the Governor and his staff in Albany. Chris Snyder who worked as an intern at the Olympic Museum connected me to Petr Spurney and shared some of his knowledge and research. I spoke to others who attended the games and recalled the atmosphere and events of that unique time.

I searched all the old publications I could find, and my son, Joseph, and my daughter, Catherine, helped me to research old newspaper stories about the games. I read hundreds of stories from many newspapers including the *Christian Science Monitor*, the *Washington Post, USA Today*, the *Toronto Globe and Mail, the Watertown Daily Times*.

The *Lake Placid News* is available online, so I reviewed all the weekly issues from the time when Lake Placid won the bid in 1974 to after the games in 1980. I also read stories from the 1932 games in the *Lake Placid News*.

Beverly Reid of the Lake Placid Library and Liz DeFazio and Alison Haas at the Winter Olympics Museum in Lake Placid provided valuable help in researching old reports to the IOC and photos from the games.

Mark Jackson at Dogear Publishing has guided through all the many steps of publication and marketing and helping to make this process so much easier.

My wife, Kate and my son, Joseph helped to review this book and suggest edits. Regina Clarkin served as an editor and made marketing suggestions

History of Official   Lake Placid Bids to Host the Winter Olympics

1954 USOC bid for the 1960 games (lost to Squaw Valley, California)

1963 USOC bid for the 1968 games (approved)

1964 IOC bid for the 1968 games (lost to Grenoble, France)

1965 USOC bid for the 1972 games (lost to Salt Lake City)

1968 USOC bid for the 1976 games (lost to Denver)

1973 USOC bid for the 1976 games to replace Denver

1973 USOC bid for the 1976 games to replace Salt Lake City (approved)

1973 IOC bid for the 1976 games (lost to Innsbruck, Austria)

1974 USOC bid for the 1980 games (approved)

1974 IOC bid for the 1980 games (approved)

Timeline

1895 - Lake Placid Club opens

1918 - First speed skating competition held in Lake Placid

1924 - First Winter Olympics held in Chamonix, France

1928 - Second Winter Olympics held in St. Moritz, Switzerland

1929 - 1932 Winter Games Awarded

1932 - February - 3rd Winter Games held in Lake Placid; summer games held in Los Angeles

1948 - Olympic Games resume after World War II; Winter Games held in St. Moritz, Switzerland

1956 - joint bid with Detroit for Olympics fails

1958 - Whiteface Mountain ski area opens

1968 - Winter Games in Grenoble, France Lake Placid bid as US candidate fails

1969 - Kennedy Memorial Games held in Lake Placid

1972 – World University Games held in Lake Placid

1972 - November - Colorado voters reject referendum to finance 1976 Winter games, Denver withdraws as host

1972 - Lord Michael Killanin succeeds Avery Brundage as President of the IOC

1974 - November 4 - 13th Winter Olympic games awarded to Lake Placid at IOC meeting in Lausanne, Switzerland

1976 - September 29, Lake Placid Olympic funding legislation signed by President Ford

1977 - April 21, official groundbreaking for Olympic construction

1978 - October 7, Petr Spurney hired by LPOOC

1978 - December 23 Ronald MacKenzie dies of heart attack at Intervale

1979 - September new Olympic arena opens

1979 - December 26 Soviet Union invades Afghanistan

1980 - February 12-24 Thirteenth Winter Games, Lake Placid

1980 - July, Moscow Summer Olympics open with US and other countries boycotting

1980 - September, new prison opens after conversion from athletes village

1981 - ORDA bill passed by New York State Legislature

1982 - Olympic Training facilities open in Lake Placid

1984 -Los Angeles Summer Olympics boycotted by Soviet Union and 15 other countries

1989 - New Olympic training facilities open

1998 - NHL hockey players compete in Olympics for the first time in Nagano

2000 - new bobsled and luge open

2000 - Goodwill Games in Lake Placid

2002 - February, Jim Shea, Jr. wins Gold medal in Skeleton at Salt Lake Olympics

2005 - Olympic Arena re-named Herb Brooks Arena, 1932 re-named Jack Shea Arena

National Medal Standings, 1980 Winter Olympics

East Germany 23 Medals, 9 Gold, 7 Silver, 7 Bronze
Soviet Union, 22 Medals, 10 Gold, 6 Silver, 6 Bronze
United States, 12 Medals, 6 Gold, 4 Silver, 2 Bronze
Norway, 10 Medals, 1 Gold, 3 Silver, 6 Bronze
Finland, 9 Medals, 1 Gold, 5 Silver, 3 Bronze
Austria, 7 Medals, 3 Gold, 2 Silver, 2 Bronze
Switzerland, 5 Medals, 1 Gold, 1 Silver, 3 Bronze
West Germany, 5 Medals, 2 Silver, 3 Bronze
Sweden, 4 Medals, 3 Gold, 1 Bronze
Holland, 4 Medals, 1 Gold, 2 Silver, 1 Bronze
Liechtenstein, 4 Medals, 2 Gold, 2 Silver
Canada, 2 Medals, 1 Silver, 1 Bronze
Italy, 2 Silver Medals
Great Britain, 1 Gold Medal
Japan, 1 Silver Medal
Hungary, 1 Silver Medal
France, 1 Bronze Medal
Czechoslovakia, 1 Bronze Medal
Bulgaria, 1 Bronze Medal

US Medal Winners

Gold
Men's Speedskating
Eric Heiden, 500 meters
Eric Heiden, 1000 meters
Eric Heiden, 1500 meters
Eric Heiden, 5000 meters
Eric Heiden, 10,000 meters

Ice Hockey
US hockey team

Silver
Downhill Skiing
Phil Mahre - Silver Medal

Women's Figure Skating
Linda Fratiane - Silver Medal

Women's Speed Skating
Leah Poulos-Mueller, 500 meters
Leah Poulos-Mueller, 1000 meters

Bronze
Women's Speed Skating
Beth Heiden. 3000 meters

Men's Figure Skating
Charles Tickner

Bibliography

Books and Videos

Caracicioli, Tom and Jerry, *Boycott,* Stolen Dreams of the 1980 Moscow Olympic Games, New Chapter Press,

Carroll, George, *Winter Olympics, Lake Placid 1980,* Barry and Wilson, 1979

Carter, President Jimmy, *Keeping the Faith,* 1982 Bantum Books

Coffey, Wayne, *The Boys of Winter,* 2005 Crown Publishers

Findling, John E., *Encyclopedia of the Modern Olympic Movement,* Greenwood Press, 2004

Gilbert, John, *Herb Brooks, the Inside Story of a Hockey Mastermind*

Hamilton, Scott, *Landing It,* Kensington Books, 1999

Maraniss, David, *Rome 1960,* Simon and Shuster, 2008

Ortloff, George Christian, *Lake Placid and the Olympics, 1932-1980*

Lake Placid, 1980 XXIII Winter Olympics

The Miracle of Lake Placid, ABC Sports Video

Report to the International Olympic Committee, 1932 Winter Olympics

Report to the International Olympic Committee, 1980 Winter Olympics

Small Town, Big Dreams, Marc Nathanson

Spallek, Edgar, Olympic Games 1980

Stephen Wenn, A Turning Point for IOC Television Policy: US Television Rights Negotiations and the Lake Placid and Moscow Olympic Festivals, Spring 1998

Mountain Lake PBS

Newspapers and Magazines

Adirondack Daily Enterprise
Adirondack Life magazine, February 2005
Albany Knickerbocker News
Albany Times Union
Christian Science Monitor
Lake Placid News
New York Times
New Yorker magazine
Parade Magazine
Sports Illustrated magazine
Time magazine
Toronto Globe and Mail
US News and World Report
USA Today
Washington Post
Watertown Daily Times

Index

About the Author

Michael Burgess grew up in the North Country of New York State. He was born in Massena, grew up in Watertown and vacationed in the Adirondacks with his family throughout his life. He attended the 1980 Winter Olympics in Lake Placid and has been spent summer vacations there since 1976. In his professional career, Michael has spent his entire career since 1976 in the human services and nonprofit sector. He has served as Executive Director of the New York StateWide Senior Action Council and the New York State Alliance for Retired Americans. In 2007 he was appointed by Governor Eliot Spitzer to be the Director of the New York State Office for the Aging. He was re-appointed to the position by Governor David Paterson in 2008.

Michael has written numerous articles for newspapers and magazines and has written a book about senior citizens advocacy in New York State.

Michael and his wife, Kate, live in Delmar, New York, a suburb of Albany. He is a graduate of St. Lawrence University.

CPSIA information can be obtained at www.ICGtesting.com
Printed in the USA
LVOW132150180712

290662LV00001B/10/P